JAGUAR/DAIMLER

JAGUAR/DAIMLER

An Appreciation of Production Models, 1960–1970

Robert Hughes

BLANDFORD

BLANDFORD PRESS
An imprint of the Cassell Group
Wellington House, 125 Strand, London WC2R 0BB

Distributed in the USA by Sterling Publishing Co. Inc., 387 Park Avenue South,
New York, NY 10016-8810

British Library Cataloguing-in-Publication data:
A catalogue record for this book is available from the British Library.

ISBN 0 7137 2713 6

Edited and designed by Roger Chesneau/DAG Publications Ltd

Printed and bound in Italy by Pozzo Gros Monti, Turin

Contents

Preface

The 1960s were a compelling time for the British motor industry as exports continued to flourish and home sales were soaring. The motorway and 'A' road infrastructure was expanding, encouraging fast, comfortable executive transport.

For Jaguar Cars Ltd it was a boom time, for, as much as ever, their models provided superlative levels of luxury and dynamic turns of performance at remarkably low prices. By the end of the decade the company had grown beyond recognition and had marketed a far wider range of vehicles than at any other time in its history. Nevertheless, the 1960s were an unpredictable time of shifting values and rapid changes of fad and fashion. Jaguar's enviable position from which to serve this eager, but volatile, market place was not coincidental, but was brought about by the skill and ingenuity of the company's founder, Sir William Lyons, and his dedicated team.

Today, the classic Jaguar and Daimler designs of the 1960s are still highly revered, and surviving examples attract an enthusiastic following worldwide. To devote a book to these cars requires little justification, and my inspiration to do so stems from experiences that were enjoyed long before I embarked on this project. A product of the 1960s myself, I have been enchanted by Jaguar and Daimler cars since infancy. Both my father and my grandfather drove a succession of them, all of which I recall with the vividness that is so peculiar to childhood reminiscence.

As a purveyor and restorer of these cars today, I am thrilled to be able to pursue a career which revolves around a product I hold in such high esteem. As well as sampling many of the diverse models created by the company, I have encountered some fascinating characters who were involved with Jaguar during the period covered by this book. Our mutual interest has often precipitated fruitful conversations, some of which have unwittingly supplied me with material for this volume.

The book seeks to cover every Jaguar and Daimler production variant from 1960 to 1970, providing not only technical detail but comment on the social and economic factors that influenced their relative success. It shows how the Jaguar and Daimler marques were sympathetically integrated and observes some of the brilliant marketing techniques which were a trademark of Sir William Lyons. Many other items of historic interest are included, and specification data is supplied in separate section.

I am proud to present a gallery of previously unpublished photographs, which have benefited from the use of technologically advanced camera and film processing procedures. My business has enabled me to source some of the most perfectly preserved, authentic Jaguars and Daimlers in existence, many of which have never been publicly featured before. At least one example of every production model from the decade is illustrated, and I believe the book to be unique in this respect.

For the past two years this book had been my shadow, and I would like to thank all those who have provided me with invaluable support and assistance. In alphabetical order, they are: Alex Antikedes; Gordon Asbury; Bob Ashby; Barrington Chauffeur Services; Kevin Beale; Ken Bell; Tim Bickley; P. Boast & Son; Ian Bond; Martin Buckley; Tony Butler; Mark Charles; Claridges Hotel; Classic Autos and Rally Spares; Mark and Roger Clover; Andy Coleman; Gavin Conway; G. C. Cox; Simon Crispe; The Daimler and Lancaster Owners' Club; Dawson Strange; Ruth Dorreen; Mike Duckett; Eagle Racing; Peter Fielding; Hedley Finn CBE; Mike and Jane Fisher; Martin Gruss; Bryan Halliday; Paul Hannah; Anne Harris; Des and Jo Hatch; Seamus Hatch; Haymarket Publishing Ltd; Hurst Park Automobiles Ltd; The Jaguar Drivers' Club; The Jaguar Enthusiasts' Club; *Jaguar World*; Jane Jeffreys; Jack Kinane; Adrian Lancaster-Hale; Adrian Magnus; James Mann; Alan Mobbs; Zenon Mouscas; John Nash; Paisner & Co.; Mahendra Patel; Henry Pearman; Ron Pederson; PR Photographic; John Ridley; Graham Searle; Simon Short; Soval Lodge; Stewart Smith; Jack Stevens; Barry Thorne; Jim Walsh; Wilcox & Company (Limousines) Ltd; Kevin, Michael and Trevor Wooding; Derek Yonge; and George Zako.

Finally, I would like to thank you, the reader, for investing time to view this appreciation. Whether you are a casual admirer of Jaguar and Daimler cars or already a hardened disciple, I hope that this book will give you great pleasure.

Robert Hughes

Introduction

On 4 September 1922 a youthful William Lyons entered into partnership with Bill Walmsley to manufacture the 'Swallow' motorcycle sidecar, and within a year their elegant carriage had been approved by four motorcycle manufacturers. Motor cars presented a greater challenge to Lyons, so in 1926 Swallow uprooted to larger premises and a special-bodied Austin 7 was developed.

Swallow prospered in the Depression, selling individualistic transport at affordable prices, so in 1928 the company relocated to Foleshill, for its accessibility to labour and suppliers. By 1929 Standard, Swift, Fiat and Wolseley cars were available with Swallow costumes.

In 1931 Lyons engaged Standard to produce engines and chassis, and the resulting SS 1 was favourably received as 'the £1,000 dream car for £310'. Standard Swallow went public in 1931, at which time Walmsley resigned. The first Jaguar was launched in 1935—the 2.5-litre SS 100. In 1937 steel replaced wooden-framed bodies and both 1.5- and 3.5-litre derivatives became available; the latter could top 100mph.

Between 1940 and 1945 Jaguar were manufacturing articles of war and, although car production was halted, the company's innovative six-cylinder XK engine was being conceived. In 1945 Jaguar purchased Standard's engine plant, but, with Britain still in the doldrums, the company focused its attention upon increasing export sales, particularly to America.

In 1951 Jaguar moved to Browns Lane and Service Manager F. R. W. England was appointed Head of the Racing Team. Victory was achieved at Le Mans, and this was followed by numerous other wins. In 1955 tragedy struck the Lyons family when their only son Michael was killed in a road accident.

HM The Queen and HRH The Duke of Edinburgh honoured Jaguar with a visit in 1956, and Lyons received his knighthood shortly afterwards. In 1957 an overnight fire destroyed 260 cars, but a vehement Sir William had the plant operational again within 36 hours. Increasing consumer demands were now pressurising Jaguar to expand further, and a reluctant forfeit was their official withdrawal from racing that year.

Jaguar acquired Daimler from BSA in May 1960. Daimler had been manufacturing superlative motor cars since 1896 and had been responsible for many of the nation's buses, ambulances and military vehicles. Jaguar's principal motive for the deal was the space offered by the Radford plant, but Sir William Lyons was quick to assure sceptics that the Daimler marque would not be discontinued. In 1961 Jaguar purchased Guy Motors from the Receiver. Established in 1913, Guy manufactured bus chassis and commercial vehicles; production continued under the new owners and the successful 'Big J' lorries were launched in 1964. In 1963 Sir William procured Coventry Climax. Founded as Lee Stoyer in 1903, this firm originally manufactured motor car engines but became noted for their designs of fire pumps and fork-lift trucks. Coventry Climax reintroduced racing engines in 1954 and achieved notable successes both before and after the takeover. In 1964 Jaguar acquired Henry Meadows, which had been established in 1919 and was geographically adjacent to Coventry Climax; Jaguar continued production of their marine gearboxes and utilised their expertise for other divisions within the Group.

In 1966 Sir William Lyons dealt an unexpected card when he agreed to merge Jaguar with the British Motor Corporation to form British Motor Holdings, but with the proviso that Jaguar retain its identity. In January 1968 he

stood down as Managing Director though remained Company Chairman and Chief Executive. Within a month British Leyland had seized BMH to shepherd 98 per cent of the British car industry, but the gargantuan conglomerate was to struggle in the economically cursed climate of the following decade. In 1972 Sir William fully retired and F. R. W. England gallantly assumed his position. The glorious V12 was unveiled, but amidst factory strikes and a fuel crisis.

During the 1970s Jaguars and Daimlers were blatantly rubbing shoulders with other BL ranges, but, despite the indignity, their overall excellence shone through. The year 1980 was the turning point, when John Egan became Jaguar's Chief Executive, and by 1981 superior finishes were evident and the 'higher-efficiency' V12 had been launched. The company regained independence in August 1984, and by the year's end a record 33,000 cars had been despatched.

On 8 February 1985 Sir William Lyons passed peacefully away at home, and it was of some consolation that he had lived to witness Jaguar revived. In 1989 Ford successfully bid to control Jaguar, but with the shrewd understanding that the operations of both companies should remain autonomous.

Jaguar have never lost sight of their heritage, and that today's models still bear a strong visual resemblance to their forebears is the ultimate compliment that can be paid to the company's founder.

◀ Sir William Lyons.

Jaguar XK 150/150S

The Jaguar XK 150 was the final expression of one of the company's most prolific projects, though the model's evolution had not been deliberately contrived.

The first-born 3.4-litre XK 120, launched at the Earl's Court Motor Show in 1948, was a hurriedly prepared, limited-edition, aluminium two-seater roadster devised chiefly to publicise Jaguar's exhilarating new XK engine.

The latter, assuming reasonable reliability, would, it was hoped, serve to perpetuate an appetite for the unit's more commercially critical usage under the bonnet of the Mark 7 saloon, which was still at an embryonic stage.

Within days of the XK 120's debut, however, the incredible support showered upon it had alerted Jaguar to tool up expeditiously for full-scale production in steel to blitz-

krieg the world's sports car market. With hindsight, though, it was self-evident that the XK 120 and its ensuing offspring would be so hailed. As the chosen herald to bear tidings of the XK power unit, it could not fail to create an impact and in its shape it was a Madonna—optically elegant and additionally appealing because of its simplicity.

The XK always catered for a well-mannered ride within an urbane environment, but to spearhead their field into the 1960s the cars received continuous cultivation. By the time the XK 150 had landed in 1957 it could fairly be judged as a chalk-and-cheese motor car compared to the scantily clad original.

It should not be forgotten, however, that many of the graces bestowed upon it were inherited from the intermediate model, the XK 140, which was produced between 1954 and 1957. For example, the XK 140 had Alford and Alder rack-and-pinion steering fitted as an improvement over the original XK 120's comparatively woolly 'Burman recirculating ball'. The engine was also mounted three inches further forward to enlarge the car's cabin space, with a consequential handling improvement into the bargain. Its larger rear lights, wing-mounted indicators and beefier bumpers to ward off minor conflicts became a must for the stiffening North American regulations.

The XK 150, however, was the consummation of gentility in an XK theme. Most celebrated was the introduc-

► *Windscreen washers were standard on the XK 150 'S' but an extra cost option on all others in the range.*

◄ *The motorway crash barrier-style bumpers were a Jaguar trademark from the mid 1950s until the early 1960s.*

tion of Dunlop disc braking. Though technically still an option, its fitment was almost mandatory. Drum braking had been the only noteworthy impediment with the earlier cars, the rears being the most capricious, particularly on non-wire-wheeled cars with enclosed spats. Cars with automatic transmission featured both 'speedhold', with an optional lock in second gear, and an 'anti-creep' device. When the car was brought to a halt, its brakes would part-lock to foil uninvited progress, yet, once the throttle was reapplied, they would automatically release.

Aesthetically, the XK 150 was a significantly transformed object. A resourceful heightening of the car's en-

tire body line staved off boredom with the XK's now familiar profile and afforded the 150 an extra two inches of elbow width on either side. The existing bonnet, which was now required to be wider, was split and re-joined to a central tongue, and a broader front grille empathised with that of the Mark 1 3.4 saloon. Bonnet mascots became optional and visibility was improved by a curved, one-piece windscreen.

There were three principle body styles: the rough-and-ready roadster, the copiously behooded drop-head and the fully enclosed fixed-head. For all three there were sundry performance packages. Apart from the standard 3.4-litre cars there were special-equipment models with a B type cylinder head and wire wheels as standard. In 1958 the S models were introduced (all manual with overdrive), with a straight port cylinder head, triple carburettors and a brawny clutch. Finally, in late 1959 the 3.8 litre option was offered on special-equipment and S models and the fixed-head was noted as the fastest enclosed production car of its day. As to the interior, walnut-veneered mahogany was foresaken in favour of a padded hide facia. As an entity, woodwork was not to be reinstated on a Jag-

Although Jaguar had officially retired from motor racing in 1957, they advertised the dates of their past Le Mans victories on the boot badges of every XK 150.

▼ *Most rapid of the species was the 3.8 'S'.*

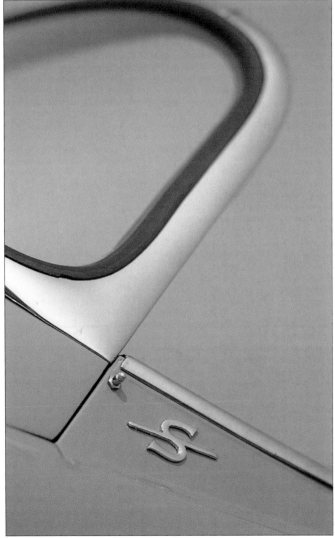

uar sports car's dashboard until July 1981, when the XJS HE was launched.

By 1961 it was time for the XK 150s to stand aside, but not because of any ineptitude on their part. By existing standards the cars still ran and cornered like greyhounds and their contouring was, from some angles at least, hauntingly similar to that of the contemporary Mark 2 saloon. The interior was admittedly passé, though rejuvenation would have been a relatively trivial task. The reason was pragmatic: whilst Jaguar had been wise progressively to embroider the XK to foster the loyalties of those who had grown up with it, the space and comfort the Mark 2 now had to offer was more empirically tempting to these now middle-aged customers. For the moneyed young man of the Sixties, the XK 150 was simply old hat. Like his girlfriends, he fancied a sports car to be more sexy than romantic, and that most cynically contrasts the XK and its successor, the E Type.

Today, all XKs are highly desirable, though fixed-heads are less so than drop-heads or roadsters. To some, the altered waistline of the XK 150 defaced the sanctity of the original lines, but the later cars are indisputably better drivers. For the zealot, the choice would rest with the purity of the original design, and for the lily-livered only the cosiness of the latter models would suffice.

For the remaining masses, however, the ownership of an XK in any guise would be a delightful experience and prove to be a timeless investment.

Jaguar Mark 9

The Jaguar Mark 9 was the last of a generation, and, although in its twilight hours by the 1960s, the breed's historical importance to Jaguar should not be overlooked. The Mark 9 was the ultimate development of a trusty format which had already seen Jaguar through a pivotal decade.

Ever since the war all manufacturers had been under pressure to rejuvenate their ranges, and the merits of their wares were more than ever scrutinised as indicative of each company's chances of survival. The Mark 9's progenitor, the Mark 7, was launched in 1950 and had been Jaguar's first saloon to break away from the constituted

▶ 121 RPA was awarded a silver certificate of excellence when it was displayed at the National Classic Car Show in May 1996. It has a genuine mileage of 53,000.

formation of disjunctive wings and running boards which were as old as the horseless carriage itself. Excepting its wing-mounted sidelights, pattern of hub cap and an affinity towards the back of its roofline, there was little to connect the cursive sweep of the Mark 7's coachwork with any former Jaguar saloon.

Aside from a more fashionable look, the imperious design offered scores of practicalities to recommend it. Consolidated front wings eased access to the engine compart-ment and the boot was both gigantic and resourcefully contrived. Its depth enabled the spare wheel to stand erect on the right-hand side, and tool kits vacated their usual haunt for relocation in the car's front door pockets. The interior itself was blatantly wider, with the car's body ex-tending to the outer limits of the previous model's run-ning boards.

Mechanically, the Mark 7 was equally progressive with the magnanimous 3.4-litre XK engine under its skin. Its

◀ *Jaguar's advertising slogan 'Grace, Space and Pace' was first connected with the Mark 9's forefather, the Mark 7.*

ability to exceed 100mph was peerless for a family saloon and it became a psychologically inestimable marketing tool. Launched at London and New York sequentially, the Mark 7 attracted in excess of 500 orders within three days of its debut. Not only did the model reaffirm Jaguar's credibility as the market leader in the British luxury car industry, but it also proved to be a monumental ice-breaker into the American market, despite the car's quintessentially 'English' characteristics.

The honeymoon was to last with the ongoing successes of subsequently improved Mark 7M and Mark 8 models, but in October 1958 the Mark 9 was announced, the zenith of its ilk. The Mark 9's external appearance remained true to that of the Mark 8, excepting an additional boot badge, although there had been several noteworthy enhancements over the original Mark 7 design.

Rear wheel spats were partially cut away, the grille was encased in a chromium frame and the traditional bonnet mascot had been reintroduced. A curved, all-in-one window superseded the original 'split' front windscreen. and more chromework was introduced along the graceful body line to facilitate more adventurous two-tone colour combinations. Post-January 1960 cars were fitted with large, vertically tiered multiplex rear lights. Internally they were Ritz-like, with sumptuous leather seats, a wool cloth headlining, polished veneers and soft rug carpeting all present in abundance. A steel sliding sunroof was a welcome bonus and always standard.

More pertinent to the Mark 9 specifically were its mechanical improvments. Although the 3.4-litre XK engine had already proved its mettle under the bonnet of its forerunners, the Mark 9 was the first to be fitted with the more potent 3.8-litre. It could proceed from 0 to 60mph in just 11.3 seconds, though its partiality for petrol was insatiable. At 14mpg it was the least economical Jaguar ever, which, in the wake of the Suez Crisis, was hardly a selling feature. Disc brakes, which replaced previous drums, anchored the car without vice and the standard fitment of power steering meant that no spinach was required for the tackling of tight manoeuvres and parking spaces. Manual cars had separate front seats and automatics an American-style bench. Both had picnic tables let into their backs and the latter had scope for an attractive timepiece and document locker. The Mark 9's dashboard was the final specimen of an institutionalised design which had obliged Jaguar since the 1930s, though by the 1960s its centralised

▶ The metal sliding sunroof had been an assumed feature of large Jaguar saloons and was standard on the Mark 7/7M/8 and 9 series. Addicts included Miss Alice Fenton, Jaguar's Director of Home Sales, who had driven her Mark 8 with a open roof in all but the most inclement weather. Tragically, Miss Fenton contracted a medical disorder in 1959 which affected her nervous system facially, and she became convinced that an overly zealous utilisation of the sunroof had caused her condition. She was a long-serving and valued aide to Sir William Lyons, and it is not inconceivable that her remarks may have swayed a decision to withhold the fixture as obligatory on the Mark 10, despite the model having been tailored for the sweltering climes of North America. Metal sunroofs (electric) made their comeback as standard on Daimler models from 1984.

◀ Crazy siting of the cigar lighter.

symphony of switch gear and gauges with ultra-violet illumination was becoming vintage. Output from the heater increased over the Mark 8 by 30 per cent, which was achieved mainly by resiting its heater box to the hub of the bulkhead. The implantation of cigar-lighters into the vehicles' A-posts were a less intelligent choice. Accessibility was awkward and potentially perilous for the driver who risked a scalding at the mercy of a butter-fingered user. A few limousine versions were produced with a glass division and cocktail cabinet, though most own-ers wisely preferred to drive their Mark 9s. Several were independently custom-built to hearses, and Jaguar deal-ers Appleyard converted two to estate cars.

By the end of its career, though, the Mark 9 looked rather dated, and when parked alongside the Mark 2 its antiquity was accentuated. The model was phased out in October 1961 and was Jaguar's last to use a separate chassis. Its towering physique had earned it the sobriquet 'poor man's Bentley', albeit a dubiously flattering analogy.

As was the case with most large, obsolete saloons of that era, the Mark 9 suffered years of dereliction during which time the majority were cast off unceremoniously as white elephants. Thankfully, and justifiably, the remainder have in more recent times achieved serious collectable status, and ownership represents a rewarding pastime.

Jaguar Mark 2

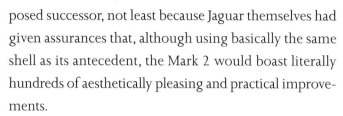

The widespread appeal of the 3.8-litre Mark 2 rapidly extended to the criminal underworld owing to its performance as a getaway car from bank robberies and venues of villainous skulduggery. By 1961 the police force had been coerced into buying a fleet for themselves in order to stand a sporting chance of a successful pursuit.

Although the intermediate-size luxury saloon was still a comparatively young concept for Jaguar, their first offering in 1955, the 2.4-litre (posthumously named 'Mark 1'), and its ensuing companion, the 3.4-litre alternative of 1957, had been avidly received by press and public alike. Consequently, there was tremendous anticipation in October 1959 at the announcement of the Mark 1's pro-posed successor, not least because Jaguar themselves had given assurances that, although using basically the same shell as its antecedent, the Mark 2 would boast literally hundreds of aesthetically pleasing and practical improvements.

To relate a few, a stark centre rib was fitted to the front radiator grille, and on home-market cars integrated front fog lights superseded the bumper-mounted after-thoughts and dummy air intake grilles of the previous model. In likeness to the XK 150 and Mark 9, sidelights were transposed to an isolated domain on the apex of the front wing, and circular indicators were positioned at fog-light level. Larger rear lights were more fashionably pro-portionate. All cars were now fitted with cut-away rear wheel spats, which simplified valeting, discouraged the festation of rust and gave the car's whole tail end a far less weighty apperance. An enlargement of the rear wind-screen and the installation of cheerier chromework, to replace thick body-coloured door frames, served to eliminate the most notorious blind spots and lightened the car's entire cabin.

Whereas the Mark 1's dashboard had been of the 'old school', the Mark 2's revolutionary three-piece facia be-came the basic formula to be employed on all Jaguar mod-

scopic steering column, and to the right was positioned either an overdrive engager (if ordered) or automatic selector. The Mark 2's resculptured front seats were certainly more relaxing than the previous bucket design, and into their uprights were stowed two delightful neo-classical picnic tables.

At the helm, the rear track was appreciably broadened to stabilise road-holding and the front suspension was further refined. There was a choice of three engine sizes. The 2.4 was a stalwart if somewhat sluggish motor, though its manual choke and Solex carburation made it Jaguar's most thrifty on fuel. The 3.4 was a spry performer and mooted by many to offer the sweetest delivery. It was the 3.8, however, that made the Mark 2 historic. The 'wild child' of Jaguar's family, it qualified the model not only as their quickest production saloon of its day but as their own fastest saloon car product until the coming of the

◄ *LPG 984D is still the property of the original owner and it has won many concours awards.*

els until 1973. In front of the driver, speedometer and tachometer were adjacently positioned and a lockable glove box was placed on the passenger side. The central portion carried the majority of the instrumentation. Towards the top was a chrome knob for external lighting, with a doublet for warning gauges on either side. Below were the ignition barrel, starter button and a medley of switch gear with underlying rubric. Heating was better but was to remain Jaguar's lamentable weakness. In November 1960 the indicator stalk changed sides to the left of the tele-

◀ The longest ever recorded skid mark was deposited on 20 June 1960 by the bewailing crossply type of a Jaguar Mark 2 just prior to its involvement in a collision on the M1 near Luton in Bedfordshire. It measured an astonishing 950 feet.

▶ In spite of its nimble appearance, the Mark 2 was about $1^3/_4$ cwt heavier than the preceding Mark 1, so both 2.4- and 3.4-litre models were correspondingly slower. With 96.3mph as its maximum speed, the 2.4-litre Mark 2 earned the undesirable distinction of being the only XK-powered Jaguar unable to break 100mph.

XJ12 in 1972. Both the 3.4- and 3.8-litre models had twin $1^3/_4$-inch SU carburettors and a temperamental automatic enrichment device. The Moss manual gearbox, with its easily crunched first, was fitted until 1965 and the all-synchromesh unit thereafter. Borg Warner automatics were commonplace in America but less so in England, accounting for just 20 per cent of the bigger-engine cars and little over 10 per cent of the 2.4s. Disc braking was standard and power steering became optional from 1961.

True to Jaguar custom, the Mark 2's crowning glory was its meagre price tag, and with the inclusion of so many attributes in its sleek, handsome design, the success of the model surpassed all hypotheses. With just under 84,000 units produced throughout its distinguished career, it was

▶ *KFB 768, a 3.8-litre manual with overdrive, is one of the earliest surviving Mark 2s, being chassis number 102. It is currently owned by Noel Hogan, lead guitarist with The Cranberries.*

◀ *A Mark 2 with the Coombs style of cutaway wheel spat.*

until then the company's most lucrative asset, attracting ubiquitous support from a devoted and diverse clientele. Appealing equally to the neophyte entrepreneur and the landed gentry, the Jaguar Mark II epitomised probably more than any other motor car the freedom and classlessness that prevailed in the 'Swinging Sixties' era.

Henceforth the Mark 2 has been to many the final word in classic Jaguar motoring, and it is little wonder that a prized example will command a substantial sum of money. Values ascend in relation to engine size, the 3.8 being the dearest.

COOMBS MODIFIED JAGUAR MARK 2

Dwindling concerns over the availability of fuel and the absence of an upper speed limit let the 1960s be the era for the speed-hungry motorist. For those who yearned for the utmost in celerity yet still required the practicality of a family saloon, Jaguar's appointed agents, Coombs of Guildford, provided performance and handling packages for the Mark 2. A combined total of about forty 3.4- and 3.8-litre manual cars were uprated between 1960 and 1967, though no two were exactly alike as each customer selected from an inventory of options.

Basic engine conversions included balancing and gas flowing, most often augmented by twin 2-inch instead of $1^{3}/_{4}$-inch carburettors. Other typical features included a straight-through exhaust system, higher-ratio steering, stiffer road springs, adjustable shock absorbers, a larger anti-roll bar and a longer-range fuel tank. Rear-wheel spats were usually cut down and re-forged, to display more of the car's wheel, but, contrary to popular myth that the majority were fitted with a louvred bonnet, just a few were requested with this feature.

Depending on final specification choices, the cost of a Coombs conversion would have added about 12 per cent to the price of a new Jaguar Mark 2. Today, a surviving Coombs might fetch up to double the price of a standard car in similar condition, though proof of provenance is vital as back-street forgeries are plentiful.

Daimler Majestic

▼ *Majestic—very.*

The Daimler Majestic made its entrance in July 1958 and was inherited by Jaguar following their acquisition of the company in May 1960. The late 1950s had witnessed dramatic styling changes within the industry, but not so at Daimler. The conservatively fashioned Majestic remained in the tribal vein of its forerunners, the 104 and Regency saloons, though, as a gesture to modernity, its body had received some cautious remodelling.

The bonnet snoop was lowered and, more artfully, its front wing line was phased backwards into the panelwork to create a more current, slab-sided effect. Alterations to some external appendages, however, were retrograde. The previous 104's neatly flushing petrol flap was replaced by a maladroit lockable cap, obtrusively mounted on the rear scuttle, and the crest of the front wing no longer allowed for the incorporation of side lights so a bolt-on BSA motorcycle accessory was expected to suffice. Air intake grilles and wheel embellishers were surprisingly not standard, though the latter were to become so during the model's production.

Technologically, the Majestic was transformed in comparison to its ancestors. Acceleration was appreciably boosted by the fitment of a 3.8-litre engine, and its top speed of 100mph was enterprising for a car of its portly demeanour. The Majestic returned about 20mpg, which flummoxed not only motoring journalists but also the car's delighted owners. The model was the company's last to embody the somewhat antiquarian but reassuring facility of a starting handle. Borg Warner automatic transmission with useful speed-hold was obligatory, so Daimler's infamous pre-select gearboxes were finally dead and buried. Although Jensen had pioneered the standardisa-

◀ The original owner of this Majestic is a lady now 104 years of age. The car itself has travelled just 33,000 miles.

tion of all-round disc-braking the previous year, the Majestic was the first British saloon to be fitted with this creditable feature. Daimler's well-mannered ride continued to enjoy congratulation, and by 1960 power-assisted steering had become optional.

In terms of its internal instrumentation, there were aspects of practicability which could rightly be criticised. Daimler neglected to supply both a rev counter and oil gauge, which was stingy and disappointing for a car of its calibre. The dashboard's glove box lid might have doubled as a small picnic tray but it hinged ungainfully at a useless slant. Oversights were pardonable, for in all other regards the Majestic's cabin was comfortable, roomy and delectably endowed with the customary hide and joinery that epitomised orthodox English values. Split, reclining front seats with rear folding tables could be chosen in preference to the 'House of Lords' style of bench, and a handful of cars were ordered with a sliding glass division.

Little was changed during the course of production, though the fuel gauge and clock, which were sited to the left of the speedometer, and temperature gauge and ammeter, which were to the right, were positioned at a staggered height on early cars but were set level on later examples.

The Majestic's glory was to be short-lived. Though a venerable model, it was upstaged in many respects by the ensuing Majestic Major, which itself was to struggle for takers alongside Jaguar's glittering ensemble. The Majes-

tic was manufactured until 1962, though few were sold and the model has sailed worryingly close to a dodo's fate ever since. Today there are fewer than twenty Majestics recorded as existing, so a freshly unearthed survivor would stir considerable interest within the clubs and provide its saviour with a worthy speculation.

Daimler SP 250

Daimler had been famous for their creation of sumptuous saloons and luxurious limousines for 63 years, so the SP 250 was an uncanny deflection from their previously trodden path. An awesome but freakish fibreglass sports car, the model debuted at the New York Motor Show in the spring of 1959 to enact a specific role for its creator. Chief Engineer Edward Turner had developed a 2.5 V8 engine concurrently with the 4.5 V8, and whereas the latter would sink nicely into the Majestic Major, Daimler did not manufacture a suitable saloon car body to utilise its 2.5 companion. They had insufficient funds in their coffers to come up with a suitable design, and negotiations had previously been carried out with Vauxhall to produce a Cresta-bodied Daimler. Fortunately, this Frankenstein's monster never entered production. Short of time and anxious to employ the unit, Daimler echoed Jaguar's XK 120 ploy in speedily creating a sports car in order to tout the potential of the engine and, fingers crossed, stimulate an

▶ An ex-Jersey 'A' spec, with 33,000 miles on the clock. The recess behind the door handles denotes an extremely early car.

continuing demand for it. Sadly for Daimler, however, the XK 120 and SP 250 were not to enjoy comparable commercial success.

Composed around a Triumph TR 3-inspired chassis, the SP 250's glassfibre body raised eyebrows. Although an established medium in motor car assembly, the use of fibreglass was more commonly associated with much smaller manufacturers. Daimler's promulgation that, if bidding for the SP 250 was sufficient, its production might switch to steel was tantamount to mercantile suicide. Styled by Jack Wilkes and Percy McNally (already famous for the FX 4 London taxi), it was a melding of British and American flavours and was designed to engage both markets. Of

British descent were the cylindrically shaped upper front wings with assertively poised headlamps and parsimonious overhead parking lights. Underneath was a very American, boldly chromed ovular front grille with chequered inserts. In contrast, though, with the car's sinuous foreparts, the SP 250 concluded with a menacingly pointed tail-end fin and between the two the 'Anglo-American liaison' was tempestuous, with a discordant profile between the front and rear wheel arches.

Negativity aside, they were some practical advantages. The absence of rust in glassfibre and its ease of repair were obvious boons, and the lightness of its structure was not without compensatory blessings. Its low centre of gravity made the non-power-assisted, rack-and-pinion steering very positive, and Girling disc brakes all round were champion. Delivery of performance with economy from the sonorous V8 was impressive, and, excusing an inaugural hiccup which saw early cars blowing their water hoses, the $2\frac{1}{2}$-litre proved to be oxen tough. Its manual gearbox, a TR-based unit, was snugly positioned and more benevolent than Jaguar's Moss box. Having long

advocated the joys of clutchless motoring, Daimler offered a capable automatic option for the SP 250.

Even the SP 250's interior defied Daimler folklore, with an in-vogue padded dashboard of a similar style to that which had been adapted to the XK 150. Sculptured bucket seats were sporting yet comfortable. There was a rear seat, but suitable only for midgets. Standard road wheels were adorned with a decorative embellisher, and wire wheels were offered for a premium. Bewilderingly, full-width front and rear bumpers were optional on the early SP 250s ('A' Spec), and the cars looked naked without them.

The SP 250's genetic disparity from anything Daimler had previously produced prevented the model from receiving the instantaneous acclaim which was required of it. With a beggarly volume of units sold in the first few months of production, the SP 250 was not to be Daimler's salvation. Once they had become part of Jaguar's legacy, Sir William Lyons was said to have been so displeased with its quality of construction that he ordered all the unsold cars (including an American consignment at sea) to be recalled for correction.

Notwithstanding this, it would be facile to chronicle the model in wholly defamatory terms. The SP 250 was never an awful car, rather one of many specious 1960s products which were culturally marooned in mid-Atlantic. For manufacturers of that era, conforming to the lightning changes of fashion was a dicey enough ordeal, but the coercion of 'export or die' to foreign places which lacked the compromise of cosmopolitanism that exists today was far worse.

Although the SP 250's rudimentary genre inhibited popular approval when it was current, its stirring design is a cardinal element for the hedonistic classic car motorist. Collectors are desirous of SP 250s, and their limited production perversely creates the magnetism of rarity. Markedly less valuable than an XK or E Type, they nevertheless represent sound value and are tremendous fun to encounter.

▶ *The SP 250 was originally christened 'Dart', but the Dodge Motor Company objected as they had already utilised the name on one of their own sporty models. Gentlemanly Daimler withdrew the title, though it has stuck fast as a moniker ever since.*

▼ *Colour-coordinated dashboards were a splendid feature of the SP 250.*

Daimler Majestic Major

The Majestic Major first appeared on Daimler's display at the Earl's Court Motor Show in October 1959, though none was actually delivered from Radford until after Jaguar had taken control of the company in 1960. The title would have appeased the archetypal, retired army officer to whom the cars may have been suited, but the word 'Major' actually referred to the lengthening of its boot by a 6-inch peninsula of panelwork between and beyond the housing of its rear lights.

With Turner's splendid 4.5-litre V8 engine and twin SU carburettors under the bonnet to more than compensate for its additional weight, the Majestic Major was truly an athlete in pensioner's clothing, which could comfortably see off the majority of its trendier rivals including, to Jaguar's embarrassment, their own Mark 9 and subsequent 3.8-litre Mark 10. Automatic transmission was fitted to all, but power-assisted steering, though always available, was not standard until 1964.

From the front, two large air intakes with inset 'V', Daimler's rococo bonnet insignia and the absence of a starting handle facility most easily distinguished the model from the tamer Majestic. From behind there were purposeful twin exhaust pipes and a wrap-around bumper which consummated its elongated rear. A rev counter was squeezed on to the already congested facia, and black, non-reflective instrument surrounds looked sportier than the Majestic's chromium bezels.

The Majestic Major was largely a melting pot of existing chattels, so it accomplished a multitude of objectives for its manufacturer. It provided a métier for the otherwise redundant 4.5-litre V8 engine and enabled Daimler to

▶ *Dr Jekyll's body with Mr Hyde's engine.*

▼ *Once the final Majestic Major and DR 450 had been despatched, British Leyland allegedly instructed that all surplus spare parts be dumped into a pit.*

purvey a more dextrous saloon than the tight-booted Majestic. The ancient DK 400B limousine had been officially retired in 1959 and, although it could be resurrected to order, requests for it were understandably infrequent. With Daimler indisposed to proceed with the development of a specific replacement, the Majestic Major was sufficiently pompous to substitute as a lighter-weight alternative.

In spite of its many talents, the Majestic Major was too hackneyed a design ever to sell like a hot cake. The model received little titivation over the years and its anachronistic though retrospectively charming body kept production costs prohibitively high. Had Daimler had the wherewithal to unmask the car slightly earlier, the latter's fortunes and those of the company generally might have been more rosy.

The model was produced until 1968, though towards the end it tended to become showroom furniture rather than serious market competition. As a point of notoriety, the Majestic Major was Daimler's only saloon to be manufactured under the rule of BSA, Jaguar Cars, British Motor Holdings and British Leyland. It was BSA's final Daimler product and the first to be struck off by Lord Stokes after the take-over by BL. The model was not directly replaced, though in 1989 the name 'Majestic' was revived for highborn American saloons and applied again in 1992 to the longer-wheelbase versions of the home-market 4-litre models.

An atrociously deficient availability of spare parts has had tragic repercussions in the long-term practicality of running and maintaining a Majestic Major; hence a large number have been cannibalised to keep others mobile.

Sadly, there are few surviving today, though the quality and refinement they offer is now at least appreciated. This, coupled with their rarity, has made them one of the classic car world's best-kept secrets. Fortunately, there are now more enthusiasts who recognise this than there are cars alive, so a fine Majestic Major is at last a most saleable commodity and is likely to remain so.

Jaguar EType 3.8

Should first impressions ever be considered the acid test of a product's worth, then the exuberance with which the Jaguar EType was hailed made the car a motoring legend from the moment it was uncaged at the Geneva Motor Show in March 1961. The public simply adored it, and with preliminary press jottings more likened to eulogies than critical accounts, the applause afforded this, Jaguar's first new effort since the courageous expansion of their works the previous year, must surely have been of great succour to the company's directors and staff.

The EType's principal design was the brainchild of Jaguar aerodynamacist Malcolm Sayer and its evolutionary roots were traceable to the lineage of the D-type and XKSS. Available initially as a two-seater fixed-head, a roadster with folding hood and optional, detachable, fibreglass hard-top presently joined forces. In either outfit, the model posed resplendently.

Though its 3.8-litre engine and Moss manual gearbox deferred to that which was already familiar on the XK150 'S', ties were severed thereafter withthe EType's voluminous mechanical improvements, attributable for the most part to Bill Heynes and others from Jaguar's racing car fraternity. The EType significantly outpaced its precursor, with its streamlined, lighter-weight body and triple 2-inch SU carburettors, while changes through the Moss gearbox were rather too laborious for a car of its finesse. The meanness of the EType's transmission tunnel sadly denied it the space for an overdrive or automatic transmission, though the latter could be shoe-horned into an outlined 2+2 version from 1966.

◀ It is more usual for a convertible to be retailed at a higher sum than a comparable fixed-head. In the case of the E Type, the reverse was true, as in 1961 a roadster would have cost £1,830 and a fixed-head £1,954.

confines of its narrow floor pan. Outer sills which raked gently under the car's belly were compensated for in their height, necessitating curiously light and shallow doors, and a transverse box member under the car's seating added might to its fabric. The entire front end, an amalgamation of louvered bonnet with suggestive power bulge and oval air intake, was joined discreetly on either side by the front outer wings. The fore-hinged section lifted the panel wholly to access the engine, its ancillaries and front suspension, all of which were bolted to a tubular scaffold connected to the bulkhead. Protective splashguards were

The model's rack-and-pinion steering was taut and of a sporty nature, yet in town it was not unreasonably taxing. A choice of power assistance was on the menu from 1966. Brakes were perhaps the sorest point of the 3.8, with a woefully precarious Kelsey-Hayes servo often undermining confidence in the Dunlop discs. The most radical leap forward was the introduction of Jaguar's famous independent rear suspension. Comprising two pairs of coil springs, shock absorbers and inboard discs, contained within a hefty subframe, it was to revolutionise the refinement of the company's creations from thereon.

In order to achieve a congruous tolerance within the car's structure, without compromising the beauty of its torpedo-shaped monocoque, certain peculiarities were necessary in the configuration of its panelwork to ensure that its centre of gravity was contained well within the

▶ E Type roadster chassis number 243 was sold new to a vicar.

grafted to the underside of the bonnet, thus eliminating the need for inner flitch panels. Excessive heat retention could pose a problem, with the car's thermostatically controlled radiator fan often grappling to quell the water temperature. Early bonnets had external 'T' locks, but by the year's end internal fasteners had succeeded them.

For a thoroughbred sports car, the EType's inner sanctum was exceedingly well kitted, though its decor lacked sobriety. The transmission tunnel and dashboard middle upright were finished in an aluminised, polka-dot plating, with remaining areas steeped in jet black leatherette. The trisected facia panel simulated that of the Mark 2, with a cavalcade of flick switches and admonitory gauges ascribed to the centre. In the company of speedometer and rev counter, which sat ahead of the driver, was a manually operated choke—a satirical reversion for Jaguar but a

47

marked improvement over the XK 150's spluttering enrichment device all the same. The sole application of wood was to the rim of the steering wheel, and this, with a chequered design of centre boss, was the mark of an E Type. In front of the passenger was an open, self-defeating cubby hole which offered little protection from the elements and no asylum from an opportunist thief.

Smart, leather bucket seats were very *avant-garde* but restrictive in their backward travel. This, coupled with the absence of footwells on early 'flat-floor' cars, rendered them a rude experience for users of a tall or stocky disposition, so by 1962 Jaguar had excavated a chunk from the front of the rear wheel arches to facilitate an extension of the seat runners and reshaped both floor pans to incorporate hollowed-out foot wells.

Lovely though it was, perfect it was not. With rose-tinted spectacles removed, the original E Types were not without their foibles. Offset against their strengths, however, shortcomings were relatively trifling and all were to be resolved given the passage of time (excluding perhaps the non-availability of overdrive, though one 'five-speed' manual roadster was eventually built in 1974).

The E Type was, in its day, not only the pride of Jaguar but the pride of the nation. Orders exceeded availability for many moons and, badged the 'XKE' in America, it was a remunerative dollar thief.

In its finally developed form, the model was put out to graze in 1975, but life was always to be decadent for the E

Type. In contrast to all other obsolete mass-produced Jaguars, it never suffered as a jalopy, the majority journeying from production luxury sports to classic investment virtually unscathed. The recreational appeal of the open-top roadster, despite this model being cheaper than the cocooned fixed-head when new, has made it the more valuable of the two. In either style, the cars are a joy to drive and, for no other reason than their abundant survival, the Jaguar E Type is probably the world's greatest-value supercar on the market today.

THE LIGHTWEIGHT MODELS

Although Jaguar as a manufacturer no longer participated officially in motor racing, twelve competition E Types were built in 1963, at the request of the distributors and private owners with an interest in racing. In shape, the 'lightweights' were matched to their all-steel counterparts, but the construction of their centre monocoque and bonnet was in light alloy. The cars were fuel-injected, had a modified cylinder head and had an aluminium block. They could produce around 340bhp. Anti-roll bars were stiffened and some stronger components from the Mark 10 were fitted. Large brake callipers and thicker discs were supplied, as previously used on the Mark 9.

Chassis numbers allocated to these 'specials' followed sequentially with the production E Types, though they are recognisable by their 'S' prefix.

Daimler SP 250 'B' Spec

Within a month of the E Type's launch, an improved SP 250 was tendered and these replacement cars were tagged the 'B' spec models.

Most urgently, the chassis was strengthened to curb the flexibility of the fibreglass body, as on 'A' spec cars there had been a hazardous tendency for doors to burst open on harsh, meandering or challenging surfaces. Front and rear bumpers were now fitted in propriety, in accompaniment with windscreen washers and an adjustable steering column. The placement of a fuel tank reserve was a bizarre

The police force ordered a consignment of 'B' specification SP 250s for highway patrol, but when driven hard their first gear tended to 'strip out' and hub caps took flight like Frisbees. Before long most had been converted to automatic and few were possessing their embellishers.

▲ In 1962 coachbuilders Ogle fabricated a glass fibre-bodied sporting tourer which, it was hoped, would be fostered by Jaguar as a Daimler SP250 replacement. Although a few were built, David Ogle was killed in a car accident and plans for the alliance were scrapped. The design was subsequently snapped up by Reliant and became famous as the Scimitar.

introduction for Jaguar as they did not grace their own designs with this helpful device.

With the XK 150 now defunct and the EType powerless to cater for users of automatic transmission or a rear seat, the SP 250's advantage was perceivably heightened. As the first Daimler to receive a financial injection by Jaguar, it was evidence of their vow to guard the interests of the marque from that time on.

51

Daimler DR 450

The DR 450 was announced in September 1961, to provide the services of a formal limousine. Ostensibly a Majestic Major with a liberal 2 feet of structure added to its rear passenger compartment, the model was Daimler's first to evolve under the regime of Jaguar.

Although its independent front suspension and lengthened chassis were adapted from a time-warped design which Daimler had plied since the introduction of their 'New 15' model in 1937, its highway conduct was considered excellent, with 'scuttle shake' barely in evidence.

As a token of compassion to their drivers, power-assisted steering and automatic transmission were standard from the outset. A testimonial to the might of its 4.5-litre V8 engine was that, despite the encumbrance of its supplemental girth, the DR 450 could reach a top speed of 118mph—surrendering just 5mph against the ordinary saloon.

▶ *FMH 375B—originally black—was owned new by Lord Cohen while he was Lord Mayor of London.*

▶ ▶ *The DR 450 and Majestic Major combined to account for a derisory 2 per cent of the company's volume, yet their cost per unit far exceeded that of any other Jaguar or Daimler model. Both were assembled along isolated, manually operated lines, and, although Jaguar had progressed to opal synthetic paint finishes in 1952, the large Daimlers continued to be sprayed in cellulose. All chromework was produced in-house, excluding the Majestic Major / DR 450 radiator shell, which was delivered by an outside supplier.*

Its interior was like a Tardis. The inclusion of twin, folda-way seats rendered the vehicle a roomy, eight-seater people-carrier and, laden or not, its Wilton-smothered floor space was bountiful. The chauffeur's inflexible bench was upholstered in genuine Connolly hide, which could be carried through to the rear chamber if West of England cloth or Bedford cord were not preferred. Front and rear had disconnected heating arrangements and a sideways sliding, or electric, glass division separated the two. An optional wireless, which was usually sunk into the near-side rear door panel, had a peculiar set-up. Its volume could be adjusted from both compartments, though the chauffeur had no influence over the choice of station.

A few 'laundelettes' were factory-produced to special order, and accomplished independent coachbuilders, such as Woodall Nicholson, Mulliner Park Ward and Thomas Startin Junior, purchased partly assembled chassis for

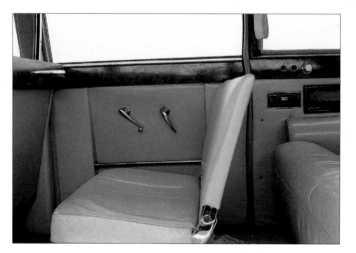

elegant, if slightly sinister-looking, hearse adaptations. Inevitably there were slight variations on the theme, though most incorporated either two front folding chairs to access pall-bearer seating adjacent to the bier or a rigid continuous bench, with a glass division behind. Wastefully, the undertakers, for whom the car was tailored, could not have savoured the disrespectfully eager performance that the 4.5-litre V8 discharged.

With their regal connections, Daimler had always been renowned for supplying a hardened percentage of the limousine market, so, despite a vital number of cheaper alternatives which surfaced in the 1960s, the DR 450's image and restrained, more appropriate styling allowed

▲ *The facility for His Lordship's ensign is still intact.*

▼ Overtakers for the undertakers.

the model to remain a prominent player in the field. Essentially, to Jaguar, the model's acclaim had assured a promising future for their own first serious investment into the sphere, with the DS 420 in 1968.

The marque is rarely seen in service today, though a handful of DR 450 limousines and hearses still exist, to provide a commodious if slightly eccentric alternative for the classic car enthusiast.

Jaguar Mark 10

With the Mark 9 the most aged in the Jaguar range, the 'king-sized' Mark 10 was launched to an expectant audience at the Earl's Court Motor Show in October 1961 and was promised to be an infinitely more advanced motor car than that which it superseded.

On approach it resembled an oversized sting ray, with an important boardroom-table bonnet, gradually sloping to an inwardly slanted front. Its roof line was far more evenly planed than that of the leavened Mark 2, though its chunky rear pillars bore the family resemblance. The

In 1960 two camouflaged Mark 10 prototypes were secretly road tested through France. One was written off against a tree and the other came within a whisker of obliteration when it skidded towards the path of an oncoming train.

bootlid, too, was predominantly flat but remained bulbous at the rear. Luggage capacity was enormous within and, in common with the Mark 9, its spare wheel was vertically rested. The profile of the rear wings followed an uninterrupted flow beyond the circumferential outline of the bootlid and eventually tapered to a silhouette of the car's gothically pointed rear lights. If a curvaceous complexion was lacking on the upper surfaces, it was more than made up for along the vertical panels. Wings and particularly doors were bloated at the waistline as if to jibe at the model's extravagant traits, and its dinky 14-inch wheels (perversely the smallest of a Jaguar) were virtually invisible from certain angles. Crossways, the Mark 10 spanned 6 feet 4 inches and remains unchallenged as Britain's widest-ever production saloon. It was one of Jaguar's largest and hardiest monocoques, yet it called for little by way of effectual contribution from its roof section to maintain its flawless stability. With America in mind, Jag-

To describe the Mark 10 as elephantine is a little unkind, though it certainly had a large trunk!

◀ Being sparing on the garnish may make the hamburger look larger, but did Jaguar really think Americans would fall for the Mark 10 in the same way by being frugal with its chromework?

uar toyed with notion of a 'pillarless coupé' version, but insufferable degrees of wind noise and water leakage resulted in the strangulation of the project. Despite the model's patrician role, the Mark 10 displayed little by way of superfluous ornament. A meagre tombstone-shaped front grille had no centre vane and its mascot was kitten-sized. Door handles looked lost, with no brightwork striping either side.

Under the bonnet, the Mark 10's tried and tested 3.8-litre XK engine gained muscle from the adoption of both straight port cylinder head and a trio of SU carburettors. With the E Type style of independent rear suspension cultivated to suit its expansive wheel-base, the model rode like a magic carpet. The majority adjured were with the Borg Warner automatic gearbox as the Moss manual selector was unworkably distant for the well-being of most drivers. Kelsey-Hayes bellows restrained the car adequately, but with a ham-fisted lack of precision, especially in heavy traffic. Burman power-assisted steering was wisely fitted to all.

Internal furnishings were as prodigious as those of a luxury ocean liner. Fine Connolly hide and deep pile carpeting was lavished unstintingly and a near forest was felled to bedeck its dashboard, door cappings and window surrounds, with choice mahogany and an elect walnut veneer. Heating and ventilation was markedly improved over previous models. The Mark 10 was the first Jaguar saloon to be fitted with reclining front seats as standard, and they were sumptuous to a fault. In spite of arm rests on either side, their sheer width denied them adequate lateral support and the driver was incited to slouch. Into the seat backs were stowed useful vanity mirrors abutting twin foldaway tables, which were size enough for a banquet. Electric windows were an innovation for Jaguar and became a popular accessory, particularly in America.

For all its pretensions, the mood in which the Mark 10 was received reflected more ratification with reservation than unconditional acclaim. Firstly, its launch was anti-climactic, with the simultaneously launched EType having already taken applause for its shared mechanical innovations. Secondly, the Press had injudiciously come to expect any new Jaguar model to overshadow its predecessor in terms of performance, and the Mark 10's capabilities were merely respectable. To Jaguar's distress, Mark 10s suffered several teething problems, most embarrassingly with a dysfunction of the cooling system, but the core reason for their tepid endorsement was simply size and image. With the aim of encapsulating a larger slice of the transatlantic market, Jaguar had pandered to their perception of American tastes, with a resulting design that fell culturally between two stools. The model was not glitzy enough for the Cadillac advocate but was to many Europeans a brash overstatement bordering on bad taste.

Ironically, it was to be an Indian summer for the Mark 10. Niggles were steadily overcome, its performance was improved with the announcement of a 4.2-litre engine in 1964 and the sprawling emergence of motorways that dominated a change of landscape throughout the 1960s made the car's attributes more pertinent to the requirements of the modern motorist. As European and American styling became more integrated throughout the era, so the Mark 10's precocious design became more palatable—even liked. The testimony to this was that its body shape not only outlived all other pre-BL Jaguars and was partly reincarnated as the Daimler DS 420, but it was also

the most influential model in Jaguar's design of the victorious XJ6.

Today, demand in the marketplace is most dependent on condition. It is no secret that a sickly example is to be dismissed as fool's gold as refurbishment would surely exceed potential market value, but a genuine car will provide the enthusiast almost with the driveability of an XJ6 within an otherwise unattainable height of opulence.

Daimler 2.5 V8

The Daimler 2.5 V8 was more or less the concoction of an SP 250 engine and a Jaguar Mark 2 body shell. Launched in October 1962, it is unique in being the first and only Jaguar design developed to utilise Daimler's own power unit.

The smooth, burbling V8 had a livelier nature than Jaguar's 2.4 but did not match the pace of their 3.4- or 3.8-litres. Automatic transmission was standard, with Borg Warner's Model 35 assigned to the task. Changes through the gearbox were unruffled and its readiness to 'kick down' meant that it did not require the aid of a dashboard-mounted override. For slower but smoother progress, post-1964 cars had a 'second drive' option which by-passed the car's first gear. The combined weight of engine and gearbox was less than a Mark 2's, so front coil springs and shock absorbers were redressed accordingly. Burman recirculating ball-type steering was employed, though power assistance was optional.

External distinctions were subtle but entitled the Daimler to express a more docile disposition. Its thickly set front grille and rear number plate housing were fluted to

595 XKJ, an early 2.5 V8, was purchased new by the author and poet Roy Broadbent-Fuller and is referred to in his autobiography.

tradition, and scripted badging was reappropriated. Jaguar's growling cat was uprooted for a smaller interpretation of the Majestic Major's bonnet insignia.

The stylish cockpit was altogether roomier, with its automatic gearbox necessitating a smaller transmission tunnel. Some additional wood trimming was utilised around the heater controls and radio housing. Its reclining front seats were of a split bench design, so the conveyance of a third traveller was not insuperable. Surprisingly, picnic tables were absent and did not reappear as part of a Daimler's outfit until the coming of the 3.6 model in 1986.

In commercial terms, the car could have been a banana skin. Not only might the Daimler customer have ousted it as an imposter, but more precarious still was the risk that the induced 'ageing process' on a Jaguar Mark 2, with Daimler badging and chromium crinkles, may well have been injurious to the 'in-vogue' appeal of the entire model range. To Jaguar's relief, the baby Daimler passed muster and testified that a fruitful fusion of the two companies had taken place. Although the model's appearance did not attract the younger generation, its status, respectability and less hurried nature did magnetise not only the stereotyped, older professional but a growing number of female consumers.

With the 2.5 V8 under its belt as a flourishing model, Jaguar had hatched in Daimler a golden phoenix. Though it was certainly humbling (and possibly galling) for Jaguar to elevate the name of an old rival as the 'upper-market choice', it was a master-stroke in market manipulation. Not only did the model branding unlock doors into alternative markets, but it empowered Jaguar to extract a premium price for a Daimler version which may well have exceeded the difference in unit cost to themselves.

Today, the cosseting and longer-term ownership the 2.5 V8s enjoyed from the sort who favoured them has resulted in the preservation of a relatively plentiful number. Despite the model's higher cost when new, its value has never ascended to the dizzy heights of the cultish Mark 2. Far from being detrimental, this rates it as superior value and a more usable classic investment.

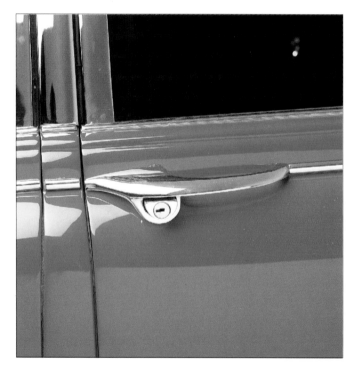

Jaguar S Type

In October 1963 Jaguar bridged the gap in their saloon car model range. The Mark 10 was proving too enormous for the needs of most, though the independent rear suspension and internal appointments it provided made the Mark 2 seem crude by comparison. Jaguar's solution was to initiate a hybrid model, the S Type, which was proffered with either the 3.4- or 3.8-litre engine.

Head on, its frontal perspective was reminiscent of a Mark 2, though in reality the two were actually quite different. Carrot-like indicator lenses with neighbouring,

CLE 945B was once featured in an episode of Inspector Morse as the villain's car.

circular parking lights were just above the slender-line front bumper, and its elliptical front grille had a bolder encasement. Thinner chrome surrounds, shrouded beneath behooded front headlights and unemblazoned fog lamps, were set like gems into the car's coachwork. Towards the rear, its roof line was raised, extended and flattened, necessitating the design of peculiar door frames, rear windscreen and windscreen surround. The tail-end itself was the shrunken mimic of a Mark 10, but with the absence of protuberant side panels. Its boot lid, upper rear wings and number plate plinth were similarly fashioned, and the rear light clusters were shared. In common with the Mark 2, its spare wheel nested beneath a dummy boot floor, though its luggage hold was 35 per cent more capacious.

The S Type was the first Jaguar 'compact' to sprout twin petrol tanks, and the filler flaps were located on the oth-

71

erwise barren vertical portion of the rear wings. Surprisingly, their united capacity of 14 gallons was a meagre one gallon more than that which could be stowed away in the Mark 2's singular tank, though their true advantage lay in the divided displacement of weight and the virtual elimination of breakdown through the common failure of fuel pump points.

Inside, the S Type outshone the Mark 2 by a healthy margin. Baroque, narrowly pleated front seats reclined as standard, and heating, if not flawless, was noticeably upgraded. The interior's wall-to-wall walnut-veneered dashboard, with a galaxy of accoutrements, was perhaps Jaguar's most elegant of the era. The aforementioned higher roof line allowed for a canny shallowing of the S Type's back seat squab, thereby increasing rearward legroom, though the renunciation of picnic tables, supposedly for the same purpose, was a dubiously expedient measure.

Refinement in its driveability was the S Type's trump card, and this was owed mainly to the Mark 10-type independent rear suspension, on a commensurately diminutive scale. Its fitment required a reinforcement of the car's undercarriage and this, coupled with the weight of the suspension itself, rendered the S Type a slightly less torpid machine than a correspondingly powered Mark 2. Notwithstanding this, the sacrifice of a little acceleration for the luxury of its silken carriage was considered by many

▲ NKX 967D won the Jaguar Drivers' Club S Type Concours in 1989. It has covered 65,000 miles.

▶ The S Type shared its rear doors with the Mark 2, but, whereas the curved edging to their lower part was attuned to the profile of the Mark 2's wheel spat, it was out of kilter with the S Type's rear. It was an untidiness of design which was inherited from the Mark 10, but it seemed all the more noticeable on the much narrower S Type.

◀ 'Ace' wheel trims were an attractive period option on Jaguar saloons.

to be a fair enough swap. Optional power steering was of a higher gearing than that which was fitted to the Mark 2 and, in common with the other saloons, there was a choice of transmission. Pre-1966 automatics had speedhold, with its optional lock in second gear, and pre-1965 manuals were equipped with the Moss gearbox. Borg Warner automatic and all-synchromesh manual units were supplied thereafter.

In its time, many beheld the S Type as the supreme all-rounder, though the model also had its adversaries. Some did not consider its virtues to be wholly deserving of its higher price and others adjudged the model's front and rear end dichotomy as an aesthetically unhappy marriage. Jaguar need not have worried, as any sales forsaken were usually to the advantage of another model in their show-room.

Today, S Types command slightly lower sums than those which are achievable for equivalent Mark 2s, though they are popular and well-respected by an immovable follow-ing who are mindful of their commendable attributes.

SOCIAL STANDING

Jaguar's competitive price edge, a multitude of new mod-els and the warming assurances of 'you never had it so good' were all catalysts to ensure that a phenomenal vol-ume of new Jaguars left Coventry during the 1960s.

The downside of this seemingly idyllic scenario was the plight of the inevitable stockpile of traded-in Jaguars

which re-entered that market once the new 'gleamers' had been delivered. The glut precipitated a tumbling of second-hand values, and many became the irresistible accessory for the impoverished spiv. This portrayal became typecast in film and television dramatisations of the era, which contributed to an increasingly 'dodgy' image for the cars.

Though poor men's cars to buy, they remained rich men's cars to run, and many, suffering the indignity of slipshod maintenance in the clutches of their fair-weather friends, were prematurely scrapped. The silver lining to the cloud is that the culling of so many has brought about a scarcity which has helped the model's fortunes to turn full circle.

The author plays the part of 'wide boy', complete with cigar and sheepskin attire, in this 1989 photoshoot spoof by Classic and Sportscar *magazine.*

Daimler SP 250 'C' Spec

'C' spec cars from October 1963 became the short-lived maturity of the SP 250. Only the installation of a cigar lighter and demister distinguished them from the 'B' spec models. A veil was drawn over the SP 250 in 1964, and the range was not replaced.

A prototype SP 250 replacement, code-named SP 252, was built in 1964. It had a broader bonnet mouth than the SP 250 but tamed rear fins. The car was retained until 1967, at which time, unusually for Jaguar, it was registered (LHP 307F) and sold to a member of the public.

Jaguar E Type 4.2

The 4.2-litre E Type, which joined the range from October 1964, was laden with constructive amendments to the earlier 3.8-litre's specification.

The XK unit was bored out from 87 to 92mm to increase torque by 7 per cent, though overall briskness was slightly arrested. Larger pistons and piston rings beneficially decreased the engine's oil consumption. Most advantageous, though, was Jaguar's jettisoning of the Kelsey-Hayes bellows system in favour of Lockheed servo braking. The exodus of the faithful but primevally clumsy Moss manual gearbox was started by the 4.2 E Type with a mannerly but still spirited all-synchromesh unit replacing it. Lamentably, however, it was still to be without an overdrive. A modified clutch with reduced pedal travel,

the fitment of stiffer road springs and conversion from positive to negative earth all chipped in to the model's wholesome package.

A re-shaping of the seating arrangements permitted a more restful ride, though they lacked the character of the original bucket chairs. The use of of black rexine was a felicitous move from the dazzling, climate-conducting aluminium of the 3.8's dashboard and transmission tunnel, and a lockable glovebox was supplied within. Plebeian armrests were purloined from the Guy Motors 'J' series trucks, though they appeared seemly enough.

Deservedly, the model was lionised, but with so much to flaunt it was puzzling that Jaguar did nothing outwardly to advertise the new model save alter the boot scribe. A rum contra-marketing ploy at the time, it was a decision that has been reviewed by today's collector with gratitude.

◀ *Triple windscreen wipers were an unusual characteristic of the E Type.*

Jaguar Mark 10 4.2

The author periodically 'exercises' this 1965, 23,000-mile Mark 10 for the original lady owner who no longer drives it herself.

To coincide with the introduction of the amended E Types, the Mark 10 was also mechanically upgraded in October 1964. Aside from the adoption of the heartier 4.2-litre engine for extra torque, the dispensing of Kelsey-Hayes bellows in favour of a more efficient braking system was a godsend. Fitment of Marles variomatic power-assisted steering partially suppressed the vehicle's tendency to stray. The Borg Warner Model 8 was now supplied to au-

tomatic models and the more buttery, all-synchromesh unit was fitted to manual cars. Delanair air conditioning was now catalogued as an optional extra, though its bulky mechanics hogged almost one-third of the vehicle's boot space.

In 1965 a limousine was released in what was to be an otherwise peaceful year of disclosures. The internal proportions of the standard wheelbase adapted well to the incorporation of a sliding glass division, upright front seating and a practical document rack, but the version was never popular with the majority of would-be clients, who still expected to 'step up' into the precincts of a chauffeur-driven vehicle.

Coachwork and interior on the standard cars remained unaltered, though a cosmetic refurbishment was to take place in October 1966.

▲ British safety regulations dictated that the fitment of front seat belts be compulsory from 1965. To Jaguar's credit, even their buckle fastener resembled more an objet d'art than a utilitarian necessity.

▶ Though the Mark 10 4.2 proved to be an incontestably better car than the 3.8, Jaguar had sampled some far more intrepid alternatives, which unhappily were never made available to the public. With the success of the Daimler 2.5V8 borne in mind, Jaguar pondered the rationale of an analogous liaison between the Mark 10 body shell and the Majestic Major's 4.5V8 engine. Although a prototype was mocked up, the failure of the project was put down to the unjustifiable costs of tooling up for the 4.5V8 engine to be produced in quantity. On reflection this may have been a blessing for Jaguar, as the repercussions of marketing such a mixture may well have been more wounding than beneficial. First, Daimler's stamp on such an aesthetically controversial model may have scared traditionalists from this marque altogether. Secondly, the 'Daimler Mark 10' would probably have out-performed the Jaguar equivalent, which could only have dented the reputation of the XK engine. Thirdly, although it transpired that production of Jaguar's own V12 engine was to remain a pipedream in the 1960s, the Mark 10 was the originally intended beneficiary. Had full-scale manufacture become a reality, an already present V8 would certainly have weakened its impact.

Jaguar EType 2+2

A 2+2 version of the EType which was tardily made available from March 1966 was the final model to be announced by Jaguar as a wholly independent company. Its principle objective was to appease customers who required either a rear seat or automatic transmission, and a sizeable enlargement of the car's dimensional amplitude had been imperative to provide these features.

The car's overall length was extended by 8 inches and its roof line was heightened by 2 inches. Doors were assuredly wider and embroidered with an audacious, chromium flash. The gradient of the front windscreen was steeper than the standard fixed-head, resulting in a token increase to the model's inward quarters. Whereas the fixed-head's roofline fell away towards the tailgate like an alpine piste, the 2+2's plateaued less spectacularly before a sharper descent.

On the scales, the 2+2 weighed in at 2 cubic weight more than its fixed-head companion, so a slight trade-off in economy and swiftness was to be expected. Nevertheless, the fluent Borg Warner transmission (when requested) and obligatory rear seat attracted custom from a throng of supporters who otherwise would not have toyed with owning an EType—young families, for example, and a mushrooming volume of drivers (particularly in America) with an antipathy towards 'stick-shift motoring'.

Although major surgery had been required to produce the EType 2+2, it had been myopic of Jaguar not to have developed it earlier in the car's production history. The car's workaday virtues are sought for similar motives today, though as a collector's item the longer 2+2 is of a lower value than the regular fixed-head.

▶ Sir William Lyons liked to work from 'life size' metal prototypes rather than from clay models, so until the coming of BL this was Jaguar's usual practice. Once a design was nearing perfection, it would often be transported incognito to the Lyons' family estate, Wappenbury Hall, where Sir William and his aides could finally approve it in more natural surroundings.

Jaguar Mark 2 (Revised)

Though still greatly revered, the Mark 2 was an aged model by 1966, and with orders diluted in Jaguar's sea of more comfortably-sprung alternatives their decision to humble it slightly to compete with other manufacturers rather than with its own merchandise was extremely as-tute. The re-working of the model was to be executed in two phases, the first and least significant of which was carried out in September 1966.

Internally, picnic trays were withdrawn and hide upholstery became optional in favour of 'ambla'. Underfoot

a conspicuously cheaper, though still pleasant, tuft super-seded the luxurious pile of the earlier carpeting. Only plainer hubcaps and the return to Mark 1-type dummy grilles in place of fog lights pinpointed these later cars externally, and mechanically they were unchanged.

Despite their relative austerity, these transitional models should not be scorned. They were built at the pinnacle of the Mark 2's mechanical development, their fleeting lifespan imbues them with a certain rarity charm and an example should be obtainable fractionally cheaper than an earlier Mark 2.

It should not be forgotten that, these days, all Mark 2s are like gold dust, albeit that these interim cars were 23 carat.

Micro blistering is a trade term used to describe the manifestation of tiny bubbles under a painted surface. Usually caused by preparation under damp conditions, it was the scourge of Jaguar's paintshop in the late 1960s. It should be watched for today on original cars of the period as the remedy is nothing short of a bare-metal respray.

Jaguar 420

The 420, launched in October 1966, was an addendum to the existing spread of Jaguar models and was pre-ordained to be the most splendid of the smaller saloon car variants.

At a fleeting glance, it smacked of a starving Mark 10, with a thinner but empathetically modelled angular front end. On closer examination, however, there were other differences aside from scale and the 420's liposculptured side panels. Dummy air vents were rectangular in shape, and the bonnet, which hinged at the rear, did not incorporate the grille and inner headlights. From the bulkhead backwards, the car's bodyshell was that of an unadulter-

Sir William Lyons had always been a showman with his choice of colours. As early as 1927, Swallow saloons had been painted in bright two-tone combinations and after the war both XK 120 and Mark 7 models were unveiled in effulgent shades of bronze and light blue respectively. Nevertheless, overcast greys and other prosaic tones were still most commonly prescribed, and it was not until the early 1960s that Jaguar's 'opalescent' (i.e. metallic) paint finishes finally caught on. Their popularity was brief, for in the latter half of the decade there was a curious movement towards 'kindergarten pastels', and such unsophisticated colours as 'Powder Blue', 'Ascot Fawn' and this 'Willow Green' were to dominate Jaguar's colour charts well into the 1970s.

ated S Type. Plainer hub caps, which were now fitted across the range, superseded a previous, more elaborate design of 18 years' standing.

All 420s were powered by the 4.2 litre engine, but with twin, not triple, carburettors. Cam covers were ribbed and of a satin finish, with black-painted interspacings. The

model's frontal design eased accessibility to the motor, hence they were the servicing engineer's favourite. As with other 4.2s, an alternator was fitted. Optional Marles variomatic power steering had the edge on the S Type/Mark 2's type of Burman recirculating ball. The majority sold were automatic, and although changing up through

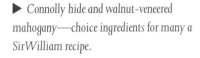

▶ Connolly hide and walnut-veneered mahogany—choice ingredients for many a Sir William recipe.

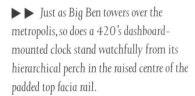

▶ ▶ Just as Big Ben towers over the metropolis, so does a 420's dashboard-mounted clock stand watchfully from its hierarchical perch in the raised centre of the padded top facia rail.

91

the Borg Warner Model 8 could rightly be criticised as a little twitchy, it was certainly more civilised than that of the other medium-sized Jaguars and Daimlers.

The 420 was fractionally weightier than the S Type (32.9 cubic weight against the S Type's 32.7), though this hardly explained the car's inclination to wear out front road springs prematurely. Another curious anomaly was that an extraordinarily high percentage of 420s were dispatched new with the higher-revving 'London Axle', which was most inappropriate for the brisk, long-distance cruising which was expected of many.

Interiors, though indicatively Jaguar, bowed to modern philosophy, with a black vinyl crash roll, with inset clock encompassing a retrenched wooden dashboard. Lean timber fillets replaced traditional chunky door-cappings. Most functional appliances were commensurate with those of the S Type.

The surpassing driveability, squarer demeanour and contemporary cabin of the 420 were all considered virtuous in its day and the car was unhesitatingly selected by those whose bank managers would allow it. After just 23 months the 420 was retired, in synchronisation with the

launch of the XJ6, though a healthy 9,800 units had left Brown's Lane during the production period. If the model had only ever been intended as a warm-up artist for the XJ6, then its delivery certainly eclipsed its calling.

Enthusiasts today have mixed feelings about the 420. Some regard the model as a most palatable cocktail combining ancient and modern skills, whereas others adjudge it to be a compromised classic. Irrefutably, they provide characterful Sixties motoring, in the most user-friendly form, and logically their values fall between those of the S Type and those of the early XJ6.

Daimler Sovereign 1A

The Daimler Sovereign 1A was blessed with all the laudable attributes of its espoused Jaguar 420, but, for a vehicle which purported to be superior, its additional frills were negligible. Logos were re-worded, the boot emblem was repositioned and the Sovereign had a fancier, crinkled radiator grille with a slightly broader top surround. Its boot plinth, which lacked the conformist fluting, bore evidence of budgetary skimping: the removal of its Daimler badge would reveal Jaguar's scribe set into its cast.

It was the first Daimler to be propelled by Jaguar's own engine, and, though power steering and overdrive on manual cars were standard, both were optional on the 420

▶ It had not always been planned to name Daimler's 420 equivalent the 'Sovereign'. 'Royale' had already been agreed upon, but Stratstone's fastidious Chairman, James Smillie, voiced his aversion to it and ventured to suggest that 'Sovereign' might sound sweeter. His recommendation was adhered to, and the name 'Sovereign' has been synonymous with upper-market versions ever since. It has become the company's most frequently applied label.

and were rarely declined. In all other respects the two models were clonal.

Despite the plagiarism, the Sovereign fulfilled a significant role for Jaguar. With little tangible evidence to warrant its heftier price tag, the model was a sacrificial guinea-pig to gauge consumer sensitivity towards brazen badge-engineering, and the enthusiastic welcome it received further instilled in Jaguar a confidence that the Daimler marque could successfully achieve a premium price tag merely on account of its name. With Daimler equivalents to the XJ not spawning until 1969, the Sovereign 1A soldiered on for several months after the 420 had been retired.

Today, the value and saleability of these Sovereigns roughly equate to those of the 420, with most fans of the shape indifferent as to which they would choose.

Jaguar 420G

Jaguar's flamboyant Mark 10 was reidentified as the 420G from October 1966; the 'G' apparently stood for 'Grand'. Alterations to the car itself were slight and largely superficial, though all were ameliorative.

A simple but effective front grille centre bar gave the car a much needed sense of symmetry, and chrome side mouldings on all but rare two-tone examples made the 420G optically more streamlined. Additional side repeater lamps were fitted in line for improved safety.

Internally, the fitment of a vinyl padded dashboard top, with centre clock, was far less forbidding than the Mark 10's previous all-timber rail. Seating was more support-

A Mark 10 in full plumage, alias the 420G.

ive, though few would have perceived it, and facings were now trimmed in a cooler, perforated hide. The limousine was still offered but remained a rarity. It is feasible that Jaguar still had designs on the model as their maiden V12, as the factory still persisted with testing prototypes until 1968. Sadly, it never made the grade.

Despite the Mark 10's troubled beginnings, the 420G had become a pleasantly enhanced model, which displayed no sufferance of quality in an age that was despairing of increased blandness and tackiness in motor manufacture. It was the Jaguar's last model (officially) to display the legendary 'leaping cat' bonnet mascot.

Its Achilles' heel, however, was its corpulence. The 420G was the car that many longed to own but few had the gumption to buy. Jaguar's decision to spare the model until August 1970 seemed abstruse, but perhaps its presence in the showroom made the XJ6 look prudent. Some latter 420Gs were sold to fervent supporters of this, the very last 'pre-BL' Jaguar, but many were a consolation prize for buyers too impatient to queue for an XJ6.

As with the Mark 10, the model is relatively impractical for quotidian use. For the enthusiast, though, the 420G makes an excellent pet, with its cardinal elements for enjoyable classic motoring.

▶ *The woodwork of a 420G is a mammoth jigsaw of 40 individual pieces.*

Jaguar E Type Series 1 ½

By 1967 the E Type was sustaining such titanic popularity in America that as and when the US government enforced stricter safety and anti-pollution ruling Jaguar felt obliged to redress the model accordingly. Although a blanket rejuvenation of the range was timetabled more or less to coincide with the launch of the XJ6, an interim model was required meanwhile. The Series 1½, as it latterly became known, mingled its way into the Jaguar showrooms from around July 1967 and gradually superseded the Series 1.

Early 1½s differed only in their employment of raised headlights, which lacked the characterful armour of the Series 1's glass enclosures. Peevish customer complaints

This primrose-coloured Series 1½ roadster is a virtual duplicate of one Jaguar retained themselves for long-term display on board the Queen Elizabeth. The car is still owned by the factory, having covered about 250 miles from new.

of distorted illumination when the covers were grubby or scratched precipitated their abolition. Other amendments followed suit, such as the fitment of dual radiator fans, to cool engines more efficiently under torrid conditions. Inside, the dashboard's central rank of tooth-

edged switchgear was replaced with a similarly positioned line-up of rounder-edged rocker switches. This latter type also featured an amalgamated ignition/starter, making it the first Jaguar model finally to discard the customary black button.

The Series 1½ became obsolete in October 1968 and today its fleeting production is appurtenant to its scarcity. In the face of this, though, the disturbance of the earliest headlight design has meant that, in terms of cost, the 1½ plays second fiddle to its more plentiful predecessor.

Jaguar S Type (Revised)

Although Jaguar's reshuffle of their range was seemingly concordant to all other affected models, the S Type's downgrading in September 1967 was pernicious. Whereas the fitment of tufted carpets and the absence of both leather seat facings and fog lights as standard issue had successfully enabled the Mark 2 to enjoy a second lease of life, the same measures were for the penny-pinched S Type merely an accelerant towards its demise. To add insult to injury, the hapless model was, for no perceptible end, the only one of Jaguar's revised saloons to be refused a change of identity.

Despite the car's wider price differential from that of the most similar 420, demand for S Types waned and they were the first to be abandoned by Jaguar in the pre-XJ6

▶ The quarter light or 'fly window' provided a useful exit for tobacco smoke and was of valued assistance to the impotent demisters of the era. Drawbacks were, first, wind noise, and secondly that a burglar could gain easy access by shattering the tiny pane.

Tales of 'better than new' Jaguar restorations are not uncommon today, with companies such as Vicarage and Beacham endeavouring to corner the market, but they were in 1979, when the Dreamcar Carriage Company set out to restore two STypes to perfection. A manual 3.8-litre and an automatic 3.4 were exquisitely repainted in black and deep chestnut respectively. Chrome wire wheels were fitted, along with state-of-the-art stereos and sunroofs (a Tudor Webasto to the black and an electric to the chestnut). The most newsworthy aspect of the cars was that both were fully re-trimmed (including their boots) by ex-Rolls-Royce employees, using materials and procedures which were comparable to those applied to the then contemporary Silver Shadow 2. Each car cost Dreamcar the then financially hare-brained sum of £6,000 to recondition, and neither found takers. Both were stored away and eventually sold at a crippling loss. The black car was exported to Germany in 1982 for £3,000 and the chestnut was snapped up by the author in 1983 for £1,500 and was subsequently exported to New York.

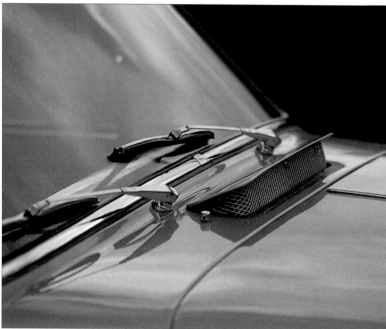

'termination' process in the summer of 1968. Their undignified departure, however, should not dissuade today's collector from purchase.

Both in automatic and manual overdrive form, these later cars profit from the model's ultimate steering and gearbox development. Ambla seating, though lacking the aroma of a leather upholstery, is both durable and comfortable, and the dummy grilles which distinguish these 'last of the line' are not unattractive.

In unison with earlier STypes, all have celebrated a posthumous renaissance in recent years, with their current and probable future values overtaking those of the majority of their contemporaries.

113

Jaguar 240 and 340

The 240 and 340 series were Jaguar's final attempt to protract the career of the long-serving Mark 2, though the role they assumed was more akin to that of a rich man's Ford Zephyr than a poor man's Bentley. The cars were launched in September 1967, and their body shape and discernibly less prosperous interior were carried over from the latter Mark 2, though the models were not just a reheated dinner. Both the 240 and 340 were instantly recognisable, with thinner, more modern bumpers and a rear valance which was modified in keeping. The 3.8-litre

▼ *Teaching an old dog new tricks: the 240/340 range.*

▶ *The ashtray was sizeable enough for the fattest Havana.*

had been officially deleted, though a handful of so-called '380s' were custom-built. Existing 240 and 340 models revelled in a significant boost to their power output by the under-bonnet wizardry of a straight port cylinder head. The 240 was a further beneficiary with the fitment of twin SU carburettors in place of the erstwhile Solex variety. It also had a new dual exhaust system, but it retained the common sense of a manual choke. Its flying nought-to-sixty was improved over the previous 2.4 by a stupendous 4.8 seconds, and ultimate performance was up by 10 per cent. Jaguar's only blunder was denying it powered steering. Whilst acknowledging that a trim price was the cue to its success, opponent manufacturers were successfully attuning many to the boons of idle driving. It was a shallow issue, for the feature was optional on the 340, and in all other respects the cars were a marvel.

Both the 240 and 340 were capable, middle-management, luxury cruisers, and their price was a prodigy. Despite inflation, the leanest 240 was a paltry £20 more 'on-the-road' than its sire, the 2.4-litre Mark 1, had been in 1956. The 340 was discontinued in September 1968 but the more popular 240 was spared until September 1969.

Although the range was a successful enterprise for Jaguar, they made no provision to replace them. Foolish perhaps—as the likes of BMW and Mercedes Benz subsequently exploited the niche.

Today, the 240 and 340 series lack much of the animated following which is associated with the Jaguar Mark

Numerous Jaguar and Daimler models incorporated a cute, if not entirely sensible, parking light, which was set into the crown of the front wing, with a tiny overhead red pip. When alight, the pip also glowed, thereby assisting the driver to gauge the vehicle's width. The feature was last seen on the 240.

2, although they are bristling with recommendations. The models are cheaper to acquire and motor just as well as , if not better than, original Mark 2s. They need not be so spartan, as although fog lights and leather upholstery were absent in the standard package, both were optional and many cars have them fitted.

Daimler V8 250

Daimler's revised Mark 2-bodied V8 was released a few days after the 240 and 340. Unlike the Jaguars, it did not forego any social standing in the company's restyling programme, but it somehow became a fussier-looking car.

Upholstery was more intricate, with narrower perforated pleats, and door cappings were reduced to thin, delicate fillets. The dashboard's top rail, which had previously been wooden, was now replaced with cushioned black vinyl.

To conform with the Jaguar range, the V8 250 shifted from double to single bumpers, and, though the change would have gained sales at the time, it was a debatable en-

▶ TYV 686F is probably the lowest-mileage, most perfect V8 250 in existence. It has never been publicly featured before.

Overleaf: Sights which would weaken the knees of the inveterate enthusiast: detailed interior shots of TYV 686F, which has covered just over 2,700 miles from new.

hancement, with the car taking on a prettier, though less masterful, persona. Front fog lights remained a standard fitting.

Power steering was improved but surprisingly remained optional, though without it the V8 250's lighter engine made the model the most tractable of the range. A superb, all-synchromesh, manual gearbox with overdrive was offered, though most Daimler diehards had already defected to the racier, manual Sovereign.

Not many more than 200 manual V8 250s were produced, and their scarcity is an injustice. Once the final V8 250 had been despatched, Jaguar were not to offer another V8 engine until October 1996, when their XK8 models were released.

Today, automatic V8 250s fetch fractionally lower prices than the 'deep-bumper' 2.5 V8s, but a manual V8 250, if discovered, will command the most of all.

Daimler DS 420 Limousine

When British Leyland acquired British Motor Holdings and, hence, Jaguar in May 1968, there were two formal limousines, both of elderly design, under their umbrella—the Sheerline-based 4-litre Vanden Plas and the Daimler DR 450. BL spared no time in hatcheting the pair, to supplant them with the Daimler DS 420 which, unlike the previous duo, was a purpose-built limousine rather than a recast saloon. The unveiling was at London's Royal Lancaster Hotel in June 1968, and this, though it was a munificent affair for a vehicle of such defined appeal, doubled usefully as a dress rehearsal for the impending launch of the more commercially vital XJ6.

Intended as a follow-on from the DR 450, the DS 420 was perhaps more reminiscent of the contemporaneously assembled Rolls-Royce Phantom, yet, true to Jaguar and Daimler pricing policy, it was measurably cheaper. Nevertheless, Daimler's time-honoured confederacy with the likes of royalty, nobility and the bourgeoisie licensed the vehicle to achieve instantly a decorous rating as a symbol of their clients' status.

Conceptually, the DS 420 was founded on the modified undercarriage of a Jaguar 420G, which had been lengthened by 1 foot 9 inches beneath the car's rear passenger compartment. Unlike previous limousines, which called on the backbone of a separate chassis to shoulder the gravitational stresses induced by their longer bodies, the DS 420 was reinforced by double box sills and an almighty, channel-section cross-member ahead of the rear seat.

Black and Carlton Grey were the only standard external colours, yet each limousine was a hand-crafted object and no two are identical. Coachwork and trimming were carried out initially by Vanden Plas in Kingsbury and latterly 'in-house' at Brown's Lane. The cars' cavernous interiors were bespoke, although most were inclined towards a formula which, to the front, incorporated a fixed, upright chauffeur's seat, most commonly trimmed in ebony-coloured ambla. To the rear, the majority were tailored in Connolly hide, crushed velvet or West of England cloth. A party of four adults could comfortably be seated along the

54¹/₂-inch bench squab, and two supplementary 'dickey seats', which stowed away in front of the glass division, were usually favoured.

Mechanically, the DS 420 borrowed all its leading components from others in the Jaguar/Daimler model range. All limousines were powered by the six-cylinder, 4.2-litre XK engine, with Borg Warner automatic transmission as standard. Jaguar's now customary independent rear suspension was installed, along with all-round disc brakes and Marles power-assisted steering.

By 1969 three coachbuilders, Wilcox, Woodall-Nicholson and Thomas Startin, had all capitalised independently on fabricating hearse derivatives. The customer base for the DS 420 swelled overnight, and not only with the supply of partially assembled donors for shooting-brake conversion: the limousine itself became the logical following car. Coincidentally, or perhaps not, the DS 420 limousine rose in price by an inflation-busting 9.7 per cent in 1970.

The DS420 remained virtually undisturbed through its 25-year production life, though in 1971, following HM The Queen Mother's request for her own Coombs-supplied example to be delivered without external chrome striping, Daimler withdrew the feature, apparently in deference to her taste. In 1988 bumpers and lights were brought (guardedly) up to date. Finally pensioned off in 1992, the DS 420 was the end-user of the glorious XK engine, which had served the company for 44 years.

▲ Dickey seats in hibernation.

◄ Finger-tip controls, but wind-up windows spoiled the effect.

Despite its gentility and traditionally classic appointments, the car's linear extent, rigid front seat and implied master/servant quarters either side of the anti-social division render it an incongruous vehicle for family outings. In restitution, however, its herculean construction and allegorical design mean that even the earliest examples are still dutifully sought for a myriad chauffering requisitions, and a large number remain in active service.

Undertakers T. E. Ball of Merseyside were the first to take delivery of a DS 420 hearse. Mr Ball's own untimely demise on the day of delivery meant that he was the first to ride in the back.

Jaguar XJ6

The year 1968 saw a radical shift in Jaguar's product policy. Their sprawling portfolio of saloons had culminated in no fewer than five body shapes, and there were six engine size alternatives—hence the need for rejuvenation and rationalisation was overdue.

Although the scheduled departure of their senescent models was to be staggered over a 24-month term, the concept of taking a guillotine to the entire saloon car family in favour of one sublime replacement was, nevertheless, a daring one. First, Jaguar's more recent successes had

been with their half-pint models, and the XJ6 was, barring the least popular Majestics and 420G, a much larger vehicle. Secondly, there were those among Jaguar's heterogeneous clientele who may not have condoned such a narrowing of their choice.

Providentially, when the XJ6 finally arrived in September 1968 it enchanted all those who sampled it, with an untouchable measure of civility, driveability and safety, enveloped in a design which, though utterly fresh, remained beholden to the principles of the earlier cars.

The XJ6 was patently different and virtually bereft of any handed-down constituents; it was perhaps most symptomatic of a modernised 420G, though of more serviceable proportions, with a subtly rounded waistline and a designedly influenced front end. The power bulge on its fore-hinging bonnet was a fortunate folly, as on prototypes the panel had been flat, to conceal a shallower 3-litre engine which never entered production.

Not doubting its ability to be recognised, the original XJ6 did not outwardly advertise the word 'Jaguar'. Only its front grille badge in an alien gold colour and brooch-like wing motifs of a 'leaping cat' portrait held clues as to the identity of its maker. Even the radiator grille was unfamiliar, being predominantly wide and of a more Euro-

TWK 334J was one of many 'black market' cars which changed hands at a premium price when it was a few months old. It has covered 15,000 miles from new.

135

◀ *The centre section of the 'three-piece facia' can be unscrewed and folded down to access fuses. Behind the spaghetti of wiring there is a small section of bulkhead which will disclose the car's original external colour.*

pean check. The omission of a bonnet stripe was a first for a Jaguar saloon, and mascots were now history.

In terms of its profile, the XJ6 was not without personality. Front and rear wheel arches flared coherently, and rear wings tapered inwards past the twin fuel tanks to a slightly transatlantic tail-end fin. In defiance of late Sixties razor-edged fashion, the XJ6 retained an inflected sweep to its roof line, though this was to flatten somewhat with the subsequent introduction of the optional long wheel base in 1972.

From behind, the XJ6 was unmistakable. Indicator, side and brake lights were coalescent in a pyramid-shaped cluster and reflector/reversing lights were adjacent in a rectangular lens.

Luggage space was a little shallow, with spare wheel and petrol pumps domiciled in a pronounced, though not unsightly, encasement underneath. Gone were proper tool boxes in place of a tradesman's vinyl wrap, yet the contents remained encyclopaedic. Safety-wise, the XJ6 was seriously impressive, with a double-thickness bulkhead, collapsible steering column and body shell crumple zones.

Irrespective of sensibility, the XJ6 cabin was anything but a clinical milieu. Reclinable front seats, engineered by Slumberland, were exquisitely faced in Connolly hide. Front head restraints were available on all but the earliest batch, and rear seat belt anchorage points were present. A thoughtful vanity mirror, housed in the glove compart-

ment, has become expected ever since. Dashboard switchgear was free from sharp edges and the whole facia was surrounded by a cranially sympathetic padded vinyl roll. Chrome instrument surrounds were not so lucid, for they solicited undesirable reflection from night-time illuminations. They were blacked in 1971, though today's enthusiast covets the earlier style.

There was a choice of engine in the redoubtable 4.2-litre and a comparatively leaden 2.8, which was developed chiefly to aid export to countries with peculiar restrictions. A 5.3-litre V12 option availed itself in 1972.

All 4.2 and 2.8 de luxe models were fitted with power steering, excepting a seldom-requested, poverty-stricken 2.8 basic, with ambla seat facings and no door pockets.

Jaguar's fabled independent rear suspension rose to some improvement for the XJ6, but the sure-footed handling of the model was most expressively polished by the excellent 205 70 VR 15 tyres which were tailored for it by Dunlop.

In every other regard Jaguar's 'master of all trades' was magnanimous and deserving of the countless accolades showered upon it, such as 'Car of the Year' and the Don Safety Award. For some time a tediously interminable waiting list to own one meant that a rarely sacrificed, second-hand example could generate a profit for its owner, but inevitably, as time elapsed, the early cars became plenteous. The Series I was the last production model to be fa-

▶ *MWK 28G, a 2.8-litre, was the very first XJ6 to be registered. It is still in fine fettle today.*

◀ *Early XJ6 models had their wheels painted body colour. The practice was soon discontinued in favour of a universally distributed matt silver.*

thered by Sir William Lyons and, although launched under the ownership of British Leyland, it had been Jaguar's own invention.

The model was significantly facelifted twice during production, first in 1973 and again in 1979.

For Jaguar themselves, the XJ in its various guises eventually became their most profitable range ever. Although titivation was inevitable to keep pace with modernity, the breed's final descendant did not leave Coventry until 1992.

Remaining current for so long has deferred the ascension of early models to the stardom of the classic car scene. Since deletion, however, their credibility has soared, and though they are still hideously undervalued they are unlikely to remain so ad infinitum.

RARA AVIS

The prototype XJ Series I Coupé is a unique and historic piece, the creation of which was galvanised by America's partiality for two-door, pillarless family saloons. Contrived in 1969, the car was the last experimental body to be schemed under the direction of Sir William Lyons. It was code-named XJ33 with a 4.2-litre engine fitted and XJ34 with the still-experimental V12 at the helm. Both automatic and manual transmissions were tried with each.

The XJ33/34 started life as the rejected bodyshell of a Swedish-specification 2.8-litre which was rescued for ex-

perimentation by Jaguar's body development shop. The larger doors were produced by riveting an extension on to the original frame, which was then faced with a hand-crafted skin. The roofline was re-profiled, and side windows—though non-functional on the prototype—were custom-made. The interior comprised a Series I dashboard intermingled with a mock-up of door panel and seating which was close to that fitted to succeeding production models.

As a two-door car the Series I was never sold commercially, though it was the genesis behind coupé versions of

▼ Culture shock. The predominantly broad-chequered Jaguar radiator grille of the XJ6 reverted to indigenous chrome uprights in 1979.

Series 2s, which were marketed between 1973 and 1977. The XJ33/34 was retained by the factory until 1977, at which time instruction was given for it to be destroyed. Fortunately, however, the hawk-eyed recipient capitalised on retailing the car rather than scrapping it, and, once registered, it passed through two further owners.

In 1990 the coupé was again advertised, and it was recognised by Australian enthusiast Les Hughes, who recalled spying it during a factory visit in the mid 1970s. He purchased it 'over the telephone', exported it and has provided for a sympathetic restoration. It survives as a manual with overdrive 4.2-litre.

Jaguar E Type Series 2

By 1968 America's drive on safety and anti-pollution was having a pandemic effect on the European motor industry, as the majority of vehicles did not comply with US outline criteria. To Jaguar's credit, the E Type was one of a minority which called for nothing by way of major revision and, although peripheral alterations were decreed, the execution of these could not have been more timely than October 1968. The E Type could profit economically from many of the XJ6's modish innovations, and British Leyland would have been delighted for the model to bear evidence of their input at this early stage of their control.

Repeating the history of second-generation XK and SP 250 sports cars, both bumpers were enlarged and the back now comprised a solitary blade with dual overriders.

◀ *A cat in the wild.*

▶ *The aesthetically polemical bonnet mouth of the E Type Series 2.*

Multiplex rear light clusters hung like stalagtites underneath, and the centrally located square number plate was fixed to a metal backing. Exhausts were splayed apart to ensure ample clearance. Headlights were moved forward by 2 inches, and a deep chrome surround secreted the rearward void. Large XJ6-type indicator and side-light lenses were relocated under the front bumper. Dissemination of air flow to the engine was encouraged by a 68 per cent broadening of the E Type's bonnet mouth, though, in aesthetic terms, what could have been likened to a suggestive pout with the Series 1 became more of a soporific yawn with the Series 2. On the the 2+2, a less perpendicular slant to the model's front windscreen enriched the car's expression. Wire wheels were fitted as standard, though chrome pressed wheels with detachable hub cups became optional. The interior door trims had

145

thoughtfully recessed grab handles, and XJ6 window winders were employed.

Its manual gearbox was quieter, and superior Girling disc brakes were now fitted. Optional power steering, though popular in the States, was ordered on just seven home market cars. A collapsible steering column was standard. Ecologically healthful Stromberg carburettors were supplied on American cars, though 30–40bhp was sacrificed. Elsewhere, carbon monoxide poisoning seemed preferable to bridling the E Type's performance, so faithful SUs remained in use.

▶ *A rare example with power-assisted steering.*

By September 1970 the last Series 2 had left Brown's Lane, though the Series 3 which replaced it was not on sale until March of the following year.

Few enthusiasts would deny that the siting of larger lights, great big bumpers and a wider air intake were superficially deleterious, but to cashier the model would not be cricket. Fashionable updating ensured the perennial longevity of the species, and most of the departures were schemed to augment the user's protection. Today, Series 2s are the most affordable of the ETypes.

149

Daimler Sovereign

By the late 1960s Daimler's 'blue-blooded' role had once again been firmly entrenched in the consumer's mind, so the XJ6-modelled Sovereign launched at Earl's Court in October 1969 was inevitably tantamount to the de luxe choice. Whereas the 420 and previous 1A Sovereign were almost facsimiles, the XJ6 and its commensurate Sovereign were slightly more transparently divergent.

Outwardly, Daimler's emphatic, vertically slatted radiator grille with crinkled encasement and bold bonnet stripe most starkly differentiated the model from the

◄ Sir William Lyons drove Jaguars throughout his working career but opted for Daimlers once he had retired.

► BPB 894H (chassis no IT1037BW) was the thirty-sixth Sovereign off the production line and was used as one of the original Earl's Court display cars in October 1969. It still attracts admiring glances.

criss-cross grille and bare bonnet of the Jaguar. From be-hind, the Sovereign was further emblazoned, with a scalloped chrome plinth above the rear number plate surround to harbour the boot lock. 'Animal head' logos were substituted with Daimler's 'D', and the Sovereign was without the shin-height wing badges. Internally, black leatherette smothered the gear selector surround, and door cappings, which were also covered, featured a chromium strip.

Mechanically, the Sovereign and XJ6 were the self-same, so design flaws which had surfaced on the Jaguar would inevitably affect the Daimler. Twin, low-level rear exhausts were originally dead straight, so the slightest nudge could buckle the entire thirteen piece system. Kinked tail pipes with an impact-absorbing weak point were adopted in the early Seventies to solve the problem. Most vexing, though, was the durability of the 2.8-litre engine. It transpired that, if running rich, carbon could ac-

KRX 512H was chauffeur-driven for the same gentleman until 1994 and is a credit to its former custodian. The 33,000 miles on the clock are genuine.

153

cumulate on the pistons and if the engine was then laboured, the deposit could ignite and scorch the top. Jaguar modified the pistons in 1972, but the engine was axed the following year. In all other respects, however, the Daimler Sovereign was a truly world-class motor car, and in company with the XJ6 it made insomniacs of rival manufacturers. Today, Sovereign and XJ6 prices roughly equate. The Daimler with its regalia is perhaps the more attractive, though the Jaguar name is a more universally recognised currency.

154

Engine space was overly benevolent to pre-empt the arrival of the V12 in 1972.

Production and Performance

The majority of the following data has been accumulated from contemporary road tests and the annals of Jaguar Cars Ltd.

Every effort has been made to deliver correct information, but a margin of inaccuracy is inevitable. Slight discrepancies were sometimes noticed when performance readings were obtained from more than one source, and in such instances the author has quoted a median figure. 'On-the-day' factors such as the weather, the competence of the driver and the idiosyncrasies of each vehicle tested should also be borne in mind. In some cases, it was not clear whether a manual or an automatic car was driven.

Obtaining production figures for Jaguars was elementary, but for Daimler this was not always so. The quoted number of Majestics is based on an allocation of chassis numbers, and it is conceivable that not all were exhausted. Moreover, it is unclear as to whether the alleged number of DR 450s includes or excludes part-assembled chassis.

Whilst the author is satisfied that the table represents a comprehensive statistical collation, a lack of available material at the time of writing has precluded absolute completeness. He would be grateful to receive any supplementary information for inclusion in future editions of this book.

Model		Transmission	Engine size (cc)	0–60 mph (sec)	Maximum speed (mph)	No. produced
XK 150 3.4	Roadster	Unknown	3442	N/A	N/A	560
	Drop-head	Unknown	3442	N/A	N/A	1,229
	Fixed-head	Unknown	3442	8.5	123	2,325
XK 150 'S' 3.4	Roadster	Manual	3442	7.3	136	888
	Drop-head	Manual	3442	7.3	132	104
	Fixed-head	Manual	3442	7.8	132	199
XK 150 3.8	Roadster	Unknown	3781	N/A	N/A	31
	Drop-head	Unknown	3781	N/A	N/A	473
	Fixed-head	Unknown	3781	N/A	N/A	531

XK 150 'S' 3.8	Roadster	Manual	3781	N/A	135	36
	Drop-head	Manual	3781	N/A	135	89
	Fixed-head	Manual	3781	7.6	136	150
Mark 9		Unknown	3781	11.3	114	10,009
Mark 2 2.4		Manual/overdrive	2483	17.3	96.3	25,173
Mark 2 3.4		Automatic	3442	11.9	119.9	28,666
Mark 2 3.8		Manual/overdrive	3781	8.5	125.1	27,848
		Automatic	3781	9.8	120.4	total
Majestic		Automatic	3794	14.2	100.6	1,483
SP 250	With detachable hard top	Unknown	2548	8.9	126.3	2,654
Majestic Major		Automatic	4561	9.6	123	1,184
EType 3.8	Fixed-head	Manual	3781	6.9	150	7,669
	Drop-head	Manual	3781	7.1	149	7,827
Mark 10 3.8		Manual/overdrive	3781	10.8	120	12,961
		Automatic	3781	12.1	119	total
DR 450		Automatic	4561	11.5	118	867
2.5V8		Automatic	2548	13.5	109.5	13,018
SType 3.8		Manual/overdrive	3781	10.2	121.1	15,065
		Automatic	3781	11.8	116	total
SType 3.4		Unknown	3442	12.6	118	10,036
Mark 10 4.2		Manual/overdrive	4235	10.4	122.5	5,672
		Automatic	4235	9.9	121.5	total

EType 4.2	Fixed-head	Manual	4235	7.0	150	7,770
	Drop-head	Manual	4235	7.4	149	9,548
420		Manual/overdrive	4235	9.9	123	9,801
		Automatic	4235	9.8	116	total
Sovereign (420)		Manual/overdrive	4235	9.9	123	5,824
		Automatic	4235	9.8	116	total
420G		Manual/overdrive	4235	10.4	122.5	5,542
		Automatic	4235	9.9	121.5	total
EType 2+2		Unknown	4235	7.4	139	5,598
240		Manual/overdrive	2483	12.5	106	4,446
340		Manual/overdrive	3442	8.8	124	2,800
V8 250		Manual/overdrive	2548	11.2	112	4,583
DS 420		Automatic (part-assembled chassis)	4235	12	110	4,116 927
XJ6 2.8		Manual/overdrive	2792	11	116	19,322
		Automatic	2792	12.6	113	total
XJ6 4.2		Manual/overdrive	4235	8.8	124	58,972
		Automatic	4235	10.1	120	total
EType Series 2	Fixed-head	Unknown	4235	7.2	143	4,878
	Drop-head	Unknown	4235	7.2	142	5,329
	Drop-head (American spec)	Unknown	4235	N/A	126	8,641
	2+2 Automatic	Unknown	4235	8.9	136	Included above
	2+2 Automatic (American spec)	Unknown	4235	N/A	128	Included above

About the Author

Robert Hughes enjoys a world class reputation as a purveyor and restorer of Jaguar/Daimler motor cars and his enthusiasm stems from a life-long fascination with the marque.

An acknowledged authority on models of the 1960s, Robert is frequently consulted by film and television companies, journalists and fellow admirers for his extensive knowledge on the subject.

Robert Hughes is based in Weybridge, Surrey.

Photograph Credits

Dawson Strange—p.160L; Haymarket Publishing—pp. 13, 14, 15T, 15B, 16, 17L, 17R, 18, 24, 25, 26, 27L, 27R, 28, 29, 30, 32, 41, 42TL, 42BL, 42R, 43, 44, 45, 46L, 46R, 47T, 47B, 51L, 54L, 58, 61T, 61B, 70, 71L, 72R, 73, 75, 76, 77, 78, 79, 80, 82R, 101, 104, 105, 111, 113TL, 113BL, 113R, 118L, 118R, 138B, 139, 149, 156, 160R; Les Hughes—p. 141; Jaguar Heritage—p. 10; James Mann—pp. 90, 91L, 91R, 92L, 92R, 94L, 94R, 115, 121. All other photographs were taken by the author.